In Praise of *Relief*

Sasha Loring's book "Relief" is the culmination of a life dedicated to understanding the powerful and positive impact each of us can have on our own health and well-being. Entirely original and full of the wisdom gained from decades of practice, study and teaching, she offers us practical guidance for both inner and outer transformation.
Kevin Waters, MD, Director, Duke Executive Health, Duke University Medical Center.

Sasha Loring provides an evidence-based and very practical guide to many different methods for improving mental and physical health and well-being in a concise and readily accessible way.
Michael Trisolini, PhD, MBA, Director, Health Care Quality and Outcomes Program, Research Triangle Institute.

RELIEF

Release Stress and Harmful Habits
and
Awaken Your Best Self

SASHA LORING

DEDICATION

This book is dedicated to the many people I have worked with in classes, psychotherapy sessions, stress management consults, support groups and workshops. They have shown the courage to challenge and change harmful and outdated ways of being and have been the inspiration for this book.

CONTENTS

ACKNOWLEDGMENTS

I would like to express appreciation for the tremendous support offered by my family in both material and spiritual ways. Thank you to Mimi, Murray, Arthur, Vicki, and Sondra Loring. Heartfelt appreciation also goes to colleagues who have been a beautiful support in my career including Jeff and Mary Brantley, Phyllis Hicks, Marjorie Scheer, Susan Gaylord, Paula Anderson, Jen Snider, Elizabeth Brownrigg, Dee Lutz, Wendy Farrell, Jon Seskevich, Ruth Wolever, Kevin Waters, Lori Orlando, Kim Warren, Janice Rogers, Mike Trisolini, Steve Peterson, Charles and Barbara Levine, David Black, and the Mindfulness-Based Stress Reduction teachers at Duke and UNC.

INTRODUCTION

If you are stressed, distraught, anxious, or are having trouble coping with the pressure you are under, this book is for you. If you find yourself employing what are called *maladaptive coping strategies* to get some relief from dissatisfaction or distress - drinking too much, eating too much, taking drugs, watching too much television, or overusing the internet/phone - this book is for you. If you are suffering from chronic health conditions either brought on or made worse by a persistent level of stress, such as heart problems, digestive disorders, asthma, diabetes, fibromyalgia, or pain, this book can help you.

Through the years of my professional career as a psychotherapist, stress management consultant, and mindfulness teacher, I have helped all kinds of people struggling with just these types of issues. I have provided consultations in an executive health clinic, a residential weight loss program, two integrative medicine centers, a healthy aging program, and a cancer support center, all of which have given me a unique perspective on helping people create a foundation of sanity as they navigate the difficulties of life.

This book is not a re-hash of the stress management techniques that have been around for years. It is a genuinely new and multi-faceted approach which takes advantage of the latest research regarding your brain/mind/body connections, as well as the effects of thinking patterns on behavior, relationships and well-being.

This book starts with a chapter that will help you recognize what aspects of your brain have not adapted to our current world, and guides you through ways of updating the system. In Chapter Two you will learn how to reduce reactivity to the stressors in your life as well as to re-orient your body for greater ease.

Chapter Three is about Conscious Benevolence. This is where the newest research is heading regarding stress reduction, behavior change and health enhancement. Learning to be more consciously benevolent toward yourself and the world has profoundly positive psychological and physical effects. Practicing conscious benevolence has a beautiful simplicity to it as well as tremendous depth regarding how to lead a meaningful life. It is the heart of the matter, so to speak.

We live in a world where we are constantly bombarded with advertisements and surrounded by shopping malls. Chapter Four was written to allow you to re-examine the persistent "wanting" mindset and to renew your deeper values. Later in the book, Chapter Nine will take you further by noting ways of reducing "pleasure fatigue." Our brains have not adapted well to the 24 hour access we have to pleasurable stimuli, and we may find ourselves worn down by overstimulation. This chapter reviews ways of finding a more satisfying path to happiness.

Chapter Five provides a range of ways to take brain breaks - to refresh this most important organ of your body. In Chapter Six, there is guidance for finding greater happiness by being less "me" oriented, and by recognizing ways to feel more connected to the world.

Chapters Seven and Eight focus on caring for your body. Presented are well researched ways of using your mind as an aid in healing your body, in nourishing yourself and for reducing pain.

Chapter Ten is aimed at helping you build your internal resources. Recognizing and building on what is good about yourself provides a strength based model for moving forward in your life. It is worth noting that though the topic of Mindfulness is not a specific chapter title, it is a very important aspect of mind/body training and is woven into the commentary and exercises throughout this book.

If you take the time to *practice* the exercises provided in this book you will be able to lead a more satisfying, healthy life. The information provided here can be a resource for years to come, a reference to return to in times of stress or illness, and a model for daily mind/body wellness. I wish you every success on your healing journey.

CHAPTER ONE

RECOGNIZE YOUR OUTDATED BRAIN

Your Outdated Brain

On the one hand, your brain is a miraculous entity. The sheer complexity of this organ has kept scientists busy for hundreds of years worth of exploration, and we have yet to completely understand how it all works. On the other hand, your brain is quite capable of lying to you - creating a physical Chicken Little scenario where it is not actually needed. Recent advances in the capability of neuroscientists to map brain activity have given us a window into much new and exciting information about the functioning of our brain. With this new knowledge a few things have become clear, and they have both good and bad components. The bad news is that some very important aspects of brain function have not adapted to our modern world. The good news is that you can actively update your own brain to function more effectively in the world in which you now live.

The Stress System

Most people by now have heard of the stress response, where the body, when stressed, goes into a fight or flight mode.   This is a biological function that kicks in automatically to enhance your chances of survival when you are under attack.   However, for thousands of years the "under attack" part of this equation was an actual physical threat - a fierce animal coming at you, a neighboring tribe trying to take over your village, and so on. The most capable survivors, those with a well honed fight or flight system who lived long enough to repro-duce, are our ancestors.   Currently, for most of us not in an actual war zone, the threats are non-physical - taxes are due, the water heater broke, your child is mis-behaving, your spouse is annoying you again, your boss is demanding too much from you - the usual distresses of everyday life.

Here is where the bad news comes in.   Your brain is not very adept at telling the difference between these two kinds of threats, physical and non-physical.   It never got the memo that our problem list has changed, and changed drastically from that of our ancestors.   If your internal commentary is saying "Oh no, I can't handle this," or "I'm so frustrated," or "I'm really angry that this is happening," the brain interprets this as a threat to your wellbeing and safety and automatically kicks the sympathetic nervous system into gear. This causes many physical changes, the main ones described as follows: Your muscles tense, getting them ready to fight or flee. The blood leaves its usual whole body circulation and heads to the arms and legs so you can more effectively hit, kick or run. Your abdomen tightens, digestion slows and the breath becomes quick and shallow, centered in the upper chest. Glucose stored in the liver is dumped into the system for energy potentially causing a rise in blood sugar. Blood pressure goes up. Breathing patterns, musculature, circulation, hormonal balances and more all change in order to help you through a threat.

If you actually had to run or fight you would use these changes, and then go back to normal physical functioning. However, we are most often sitting at a desk or on a couch, no physical action required, so we stew in a self-made chemical soup. If this happens often enough, and for many of us this is a routine daily occurrence, we are headed for a stress induced or effected chronic condition - heart disease, digestive disorder, diabetes, fibromyalgia, chronic pain, high blood pressure, asthma, or TMJ.

We hear a lot about the fight or flight reaction just described (the response of the sympathetic nervous system to a threat), but we don't hear that much about its counterpart - *rest and recuperation*, or the para-sympathetic aspect of the autonomic nervous system. The autonomic aspect of this dynamic means that it is happening by itself, without your conscious input. This is key, as it is by becoming *consciously aware* of the two aspects of your nervous system and actively working to disengage one and engage the other, that you can save your health, wellbeing and possibly your life.

Learn to Switch Systems
Much of the information in this book is aimed at helping you take charge of what is usually happening automatically, out of your conscious awareness. As described in the previous section, your autonomic nervous system is wired to engage the stress response (sympathetic branch of the nervous system) when it senses any threat. When it is chronically engaged it is likely to not only lead to physical and mental distress, it also creates a fertile ground for illness to occur. If we recognize the stress section of our brain is "lit up" when there is no physical threat to fight off, we can actively switch over to the other branch of the autonomic nervous system, the *rest and recuperation system*. This is where we should be spending most of our time, and this is the optimal aspect of our nervous system for facing non-physical challenges.

The Key to Success
There is one section of your body that is key to switching systems. It is rarely noticed and most people have no idea what it looks like. Any guesses? The body part that is the key to success in actively taking charge of regulating your physiology is your diaphragm. The diaphragm is a large, flat structure of muscle and fibrous tissue between your thoracic cavity and the abdomen that allows you to breathe, since your lungs do not have the capability to move themselves. I learned this as a child when someone kicked me in the stomach, and I couldn't breathe until my diaphragm started working again. When we are stressed, the abdomen tightens, the diaphragm gets

"frozen" and it stops working properly, leading to the shallow breathing mentioned earlier.

The diaphragm also effects all the organs surrounding it. When working properly, as it moves up and down it massages the heart, as well as all the organs connected to digestion. It wraps around the gullet, and is connected to your ribs and lumbar spine. If you watch a baby breathing as it sleeps you will see the abdomen rising and falling and may also notice the gentle rocking of the lower back. This is the natural and healthy way to breathe. However, most people I know lead stressed and hurried lives and have habitually tight abdomens, thus inhibiting the normal movement of the diaphragm. This deprives the essential organs of the circulation of oxygen and nourishment they require to be healthy. The diaphragm is also involved in non-respiratory functions such as preventing acid reflux and helping to eliminate feces and urine from the body by increasing intra-abdominal pressure.

Exercise: Paying Attention

Your diaphragm is very responsive to your mind, and paying attention in a deliberate way can reverse the stress response, coaxing your body into the rest and recuperation mode.

- The first step is to spend a few minutes simply noticing how you are currently breathing. What part of your body moves when you take a normal breath? Put one hand on your upper chest and one hand on your abdomen. Spend a few moments noticing what is moving as you breathe normally.

- If your abdomen is not engaged - if it is not gently expanding and contracting - see if you can increase its participation by consciously softening and relaxing the muscles in your abdomen. This allows the breath to drop into its natural place and the diaphragm to move freely. Then you can feel the breath move through all three essential parts - the upper chest, the lower chest, and the belly.

- Practice this breathing as a progression - air into the upper chest, then the lower chest, and finally the abdomen. Then, release the breath first in the abdomen, then the lower chest, and finally the upper chest. Putting one hand on your belly and one on your chest will help you practice.

- When this three tiered breath becomes natural, you can add allowing your lower back to gently rock as you breathe in and out. In addition to helping you freely breathe, this is an excellent way of soothing back pain.

Depending on how frozen and tight your abdomen is, freeing the breath may take some time and practice, but it is well worth it.

Another easy to learn breath practice that can quickly bring down your stress level is called *square breathing*. This involves regulating and equalizing each in and out breath as well as the space between breaths. This serves several purposes. When you change your focus from whatever is distressing you to regulating your breath you automatically switch the area of your brain that gets engaged - away from the stress centers and toward sensory awareness. As you attend to your body with this style of breathing it will also release the areas holding tension, and reverse the shallow breathing related to stress.

Exercise: Square Breathing for Stress Reduction

- First just notice your current breathing pattern for a moment. Follow each breath, noticing where it goes and what is moving as you breathe.

- Then begin counting to four as you breathe in.

- Count to four as you hold your breath.

- Count to four as you release your breath.

- Count to four before you breathe in.

- Keep doing this in a relaxed way as long as it feels like it is helping you calm down.

Feel free to change the number you use (to 3 or 5 for example) to suit yourself, but try to keep all four parts of one breath cycle even. This is no time to be a perfectionist - it will come more naturally the more you practice.

Exercise: Slow Breathing Practice

At some time in your life you have probably experienced the positive effects of slowing down your breathing. To slow your breath in a more conscious and precise manner try this exercise and note the effects on your state of relaxation. Look at a clock to get an idea of breath length. See if you can slow your breath to 6 breaths per minute, which is an inhalation and exhalation about every 10 seconds. After you get a feel for it, see if you can make the inhalations and exhalations about the same length - so about 5 seconds each. Practice for whatever length of time feels good to you. Again, this is no time to be a perfectionist - get the general idea and do what feels comforting.

Reduce Fear Reactivity
It is important to recognize when you are making decisions out of fear, anxiety or insecurity. Again this is referring to times when there is no physical threat or

verbal abuse. Once you recognize that the wrong part of your brain is dominating the inner conversation, *take a deliberate pause*. Perhaps go outside, take a nap, do the breath practices taught in the previous sections, or participate in a recreational activity.

Taking a deliberate pause will allow two other aspects of your mind to get involved. The first is what is called the *executive function* part of the brain, the more rational aspect, which can give you a broader perspective, less based on emotions. The second aspect is your *insight/ intuition*, which can take you beyond the limits of your habitual thought processes altogether. This more likely to be accessible if you are relaxed and at ease. The information in Chapter Two can also help you learn to navigate your brain more successfully.

CHAPTER TWO

REDUCE DISTRESS

Your Mind is Key

If you were paying close attention to the Your Outdated Brain section of Chapter one, you may have noticed that *it is the mind that drives the stress response.* This is a very significant realization. If your mind did not classify an event as threatening and respond with worry and anxiety, the body would have no reason to become tense and engage the stress response. Therefore, to truly reduce distress, you have to do something about your mind.

Steps to Reduce Reactivity

It is worth mentioning again, that if you are actually facing a real physical threat, you want a finely tuned stress response to be engaged, to help you get away from or fight off any harmful attack. However if you are worrying about a project due next week, engaging the stress response is unnecessary and harmful to your health. What follows are three important steps to help you self-regulate your own body and mind. The first, *Stop, Listen and Name*, is a mindfulness practice that will diminish your habitual responses by allowing you to consciously tune in to the undercurrent of thoughts and feelings you experience. The second step, Outwit Your Brain, is an opportunity to deliberately change what part of your brain is engaged. Then the Embodiment section provides a series of exercises to allow your body to positively influence your mind.

Step 1. Stop, Listen, and Name

We get so used to our mind constantly chatting away that we rarely stop to really listen in on what the commentary is actually saying. For example, you are driving to work and traffic has slowed to a crawl. It is apparent you are not getting to work on time, and your mind goes into high gear. "Oh no, I can't be late, the meeting starts right at nine!" If you are a professional level worrier you will start adding to your discomfort by thinking of all the bad things that could occur as a result of being late, maybe tightening your fists around the steering wheel and cursing out loud.

The suggestion with *Stop, Listen, and Name* is to make a habit of consciously listening to your self talk, rather than mindlessly letting it run on (thus intensifying your stress reaction). When you listen in, you are then able to identify, or name, what you are feeling. In the case of being stuck in traffic, you might hear the worrying commentary and state to yourself "I feel anxious."

This simple process of identifying what you are feeling *in and of itself* reduces the activity in the brain's stress response regions and allows you to step back from the process enough to engage the more rational parts of your brain.

Step 2. Outwit Your Brain

In the earlier discussions about the stress response it was noted that there are parts of your brain that are constantly scanning the world for potential threats to your wellbeing (the amygdala). When such a threat comes to light, this part of your brain gets to take command, and start doing whatever it thinks is necessary to assure your survival. You will recall that it reacts to nonphysical threats in the same way it prepares for an actual attack, which in our current circumstances creates an unnecessary strain on your body.

You have already learned several breathing practices that can be a great help in this situation and are recommended as an initial activity for shifting your state of mind and body in a positive direction. In addition to breathing techniques, Step 2 provides other options for actually changing which part of your brain is engaged. Training in the following methods will allow you much healthier and more relaxed modalities for interacting with your world.

Your Brain on Pleasure

Your brain is trying to help you survive. You have lived long enough to read this so it must have at least some skill in this area. However, there are certain ways your brain sorts and stores information that have a down side.

You tend to really take notice when something negative is happening to you, and your brain feels quite obliged to store this information in order to help you avoid such things in the future. The same process does not happen when pleasant events are occurring unless they are fairly monumental (weddings and vacations for example).

Having a nice day is not on the list of things essential to your survival, so small pleasures are not automatically registered and stored. The smell of jasmine as you stroll through a garden, a soft breeze that relieves a steamy day, a kind word from a fellow worker, your spouse making a meal for you .... These are barely registered *unless you purposely pay attention to them for at least 10 seconds.*

There are countless opportunities to feel pleasure that usually go unnoticed. Spend at least one day actively noticing the ordinary pleasures in your life. Some additional examples could include feeling your shoulders relax as you take a walk, hearing a bird sing, smiling or joking with a co-worker or friend, putting on a clean pair of socks, touching a loved one, petting a dog or cat, or recalling a pleasant event. If you wake up to this seemingly small but actually life altering dynamic you can change how you perceive the world in a very positive way.

Exercise: Notice Pleasure

- Prime yourself for remembering to notice pleasure by placing notes on your refrigerator, desk, dashboard, and calendar.

- When you notice something pleasant occurring, deliberately pay attention for at least 10 seconds.

- Take note of your mood through the day.

- At the end of the day see if you can remember the pleasant events you experienced.

Another way of noticing pleasure is to pay attention to *positive anticipation.* If you have a vacation or event you are looking forward to, recognize that anticipation is one of the most pleasant parts of a future happening, and relish imagining the things you will be doing.

Once you have created a new habit of noticing everyday pleasures it can enhance your feelings of wellbeing and ease. When you are distressed, your mind tends to narrow its focus to the problem at hand. Consciously *expand* your attention to include something likable in your surroundings such as an attractive color, an enjoyable picture, or a friendly face. This will relax your mind enough for you to be able to be more creative in your responses.

Positive Distraction

Positive distraction means using those times when you are trapped in some frustrating circumstance beyond your control as an opportunity rather than as an annoyance. When you are standing in the slowest line at the store, or in an extremely tedious meeting, your mind tends to go on and on about how you would like to be almost anywhere else, about how this event is somehow personally insulting, and about how you are trapped in a circumstance that *should be different than it is*. This last, by the way, is a major clue to wellbeing - catching your mind telling you that things "should" be different. The meeting leader *should* know how to make a proper agenda, the state *should* have widened this road by now, my spouse *should* be more mature, and so on. I personally have found that when I fight with reality, reality pretty consistently has the upper hand. A phrase like *"It is like this,"* along with a clear observation of a situation is very illuminating and can provide clarity regarding whether it is in your control or not and about how you could proceed if something can be done.

When the inevitable minor frustrating situations of life have you trapped, you will notice your mind going into resistance mode, which leads to your body tensing up. One of the options to change your state of mind is to make a different choice and apply positive distraction.

Exercise: Choose Your Response

The next time you are in a difficult situation such as a traffic jam, experiment with making a different choice. Do step one - Stop, Listen, and Name - and note to yourself what you feel (probably anxious and/or annoyed). You are in a situation that is out of your control, so the only place where you have consider-able influence is your own mind.

It is your choice - do you want to spend your time pointlessly fretting or are you willing to try something new? "I have identified that I feel anxious and annoyed, which is very uncomfortable. I know that I can't do anything about the external situation, so this could be a perfect opportunity to practice a change in attitude."

Now you can choose to actively focus on something pleasant - relax your breathing pattern, tune in to music you enjoy, watch cloud patterns, think about something helpful you could do for someone else, or imagine a creative project for yourself.

After focusing your attention on one or more of these ways of changing your response to a situation, check in with your body. Note the changes in your level of mental and physical discomfort. Think in terms of percentages rather than "all or nothing." Can you lower your level of tension by ten percent, or perhaps even more? That is a great start. Appreciate yourself for consciously responding rather than being swept away by habitual reactions.

Kindness

Applying kindness is another method for changing your mind state in a positive direction. I had such an opportunity recently while standing in line at the grocery store. As I'm observing the cashier I notice that I'm getting tense. The woman ringing up groceries is unsmiling and my brain is interpreting her appearance and gestures as impatient and unfriendly. A stream of thoughts start arising about how this is not appropriate for someone in a service job, that I deserve to be treated in a more kindly manner, and about how I should report her to the manager. My irritation is building because it is so well fed by my own running commentary. My chest is tight, and I have adopted an impatient and unfriendly manner myself.

It eventually dawns on me, just as it is my turn to start placing my items on the counter, that I have created my own misery, again, and that I can turn it around. I change my attentional focus, bringing my awareness out of my head and down into my chest. I'd like my heart to be happy, and the quickest way, in this situation to bring that about is to first wish myself well and to then extend that out to my compatriot in this drama. I sincerely hope that she will begin having a better day, and I smile at her.

Even without saying anything, by the end of our transaction she has visibly relaxed and is noticeably more cheerful. I certainly am.

This everyday occurrence is a very typical example of how an outdated brain pattern, when left on its own can contribute to the tremendous increase in chronic stress experienced in our culture. Even though there was no physical threat to me, and very little likelihood that this cashier would harm me in any way, my brain sensed a potential negative event - and immediately started a physiological response. Once again my outdated brain was confusing a psychological irritant with an actual threat to my wellbeing or a potential physical harm and was gearing up to defend myself, punch someone or to race away.

You may be surprised at the number of times this kind of event happens to you throughout your day. The more sensitive you become to subtle changes in your thought patterns and their effects on your body, the more likely it will be that you can reverse the stress response. Recognizing the stress response and reversing the process has the potential to save you from any number of stress related chronic conditions.

Exercise: Practice Random Kindness

Look for an ordinary situation that you find irritating

similar to the grocery line event described previously. See if you can reverse your response to one of extending thoughts of kindness. Notice the effects on yourself.

Examples of Random Kindness:
- Choose a co-worker who irritates you and deliberately look for something they do well. Compliment them.

- Look for strengths or positive qualities in a family member and mention it.

- Express gratitude for natural phenomena that keep you alive - food, water, trees, and so on.

- Give an unexpected gift to someone.

Spacious Boredom
We live in a society where distraction is the norm. Even something as simple as standing in a bank line seems to require a large screen with flashing information or news to distract us from a moment of, heaven forbid, boredom. It is helpful to distinguish what I call *spacious boredom* from what we usually experience - *claustrophobic boredom.* Claustrophobic boredom is our somewhat childish need to be constantly entertained and to feel quite put out when there is not something engaging to do every moment of our day. We are either speeding along, or flopped down in a fog or in sleep. We have very little experience with feeling relaxed, open and interested when "nothing" is going on. In fact, you may notice a

subtle moment of panic when you don't have your usual psychological props. Being courageous enough to face this panic without jumping up to find something to do will increase your self awareness and bring a new sense of confidence.

Exercise: Practice Spacious Boredom

When you notice a bored, irritated feeling, experiment with simply relaxing into your experience. Feel your whole body, and then the space around your body. Notice your senses, each in turn - hearing, smelling, seeing, touching (touching in this context means noting whatever your body is standing or sitting on). Spend a few minutes being simply open to *stillness and sensation*. Notice the qualities of your mind when you are not busy. Can you stay with it and investigate?

Resourcefulness
Resourcefulness is one of the most underrated markers of intelligence we have. Being resourceful means you are able to meet new and possibly difficult situations as they arise and to find creative solutions. If you think about it, you will recognize that you have survived through countless challenges in your life because you have figured out some way of resolving them. The most savvy of the executives I counsel have figured this out, and it

greatly reduces the need to worry about unknown future events (which is different than planning for the future). We live in a rapidly changing world which results in uncertainty about what may arise in our future. Recognizing your own resourcefulness will help you diminish the edginess that comes with uncertainty. Consider your own life.   You probably don't even remember many of the things you were stressing about last year because you have gotten through them.

Mindfulness is a big part of resourcefulness. *Mindfulness* means attending to the present moment with a nonjudgmental, engaged attitude.   There are several aspects or foundations of mindfulness.   Throughout this book, three of these qualities are discussed - mindfulness of body, mindfulness of feelings, and mindfulness of mind. According to the great Tibetan meditation master Chogyam Trungpa, Rinpoche, there is another foundation called *mindfulness of life*.   Mindfulness of life is the experience of recognizing that you have already survived. You are here, so you can relax about that, and actually be simply present without such intense concern for your future. In this moment you could just be present, at ease. Perhaps you could enjoy the pleasure of simply being alive as a breathing, sensing, aware human.

Most of the time, when we are fretting and distressed we are actually just sitting in a room.   The dense cloud of distress is self-created. So, when you notice your mind being captured by either a vague uneasiness about the future, or specific concerns about upcoming events, recall your resourcefulness and see how much of the worry can be let go. You might create a phrase that reminds you of your resourcefulness such as *"I have been successful in many situations and have confidence in my abilities."*

Imagery

If worry is a persistent part of your mental make-up, imagery can be a powerful way to change an ingrained brain pattern. Worry is actually a problem with your imagination. Worry means you are getting very creative imagining what *might* be going wrong. This is different than fear, which tends to be more focused in the present. The images you create when worrying can be quite powerful. Think about how reactive you become to the scenes from an engaging movie. Even though it is just a picture on a screen you might literally find your breath has stopped in response to a vivid crash scene, for example. Your mind is just as powerful in creating inner scenarios. Recognizing this, instead of worrying about things that are either out of your control or not actually occurring, learn to use your innate capacity to imagine as an aid for yourself.

What would it be like to imagine getting it right, enjoying your day, or creating a more positive response to a negative situation? Feel free to fantasize. This is what successful athletes do. They imagine hitting the ball just right, running at their top speed, making the touchdown pass, and so on. *The more relaxed you become, the more likely it will be that you will have new insights and think of more creative possibilities.*

For times when you are worrying about something that you can actually have an effect on, do what you can to have that effect, and then let go of the worry and practice envisioning positive outcomes.

Step 3: Become More Embodied

This section will help you become more body aware. This means purposely training yourself to be naturally aware of how you are sitting, standing and walking. This will help you experience less self-induced fatigue and allow you to be more in touch with how you are either obstructing your energy flow or are helping it to move freely within your body.

Grounding

All of us have a very profound and omnipresent support that is largely ignored. This support is the ground, the earth itself. Most of us spend our days focused above our shoulders, largely ignoring the rest of our body, which tags along behind our thrust out chin. We use up considerable energy unnecessarily by ignoring the support offered by the earth. When we sit, stand or walk, being actively conscious of the ground and our body balanced on this ground can create a rich new source of both energy and relaxation. To explore this further, try the following exercises:

Exercise: Standing and Walking

- Stand on a flat surface either barefoot or wearing flat shoes.

- Notice where your feet feel the most pressure.

- Lean your body slightly forward, then backwards, to the left, and then to the right. Find a balance point where you feel the most supported and you are using your whole right and left foot.

- Imagine your energy reaching down into the earth, somewhat like growing supportive roots into the ground. *Feel* how your skeleton and muscles can adjust to take full advantage of this new grounded support, and become more and more balanced and at ease.

- Allow your knees to be soft, drop your shoulders, and tuck your chin slightly to release the muscles in the back of your neck.

- *Feel* your breath moving in your body as it relaxes further and further. If your head tries to regain dominance, simply bring your attention back to your feet and their connection to the ground.

- When you feel well grounded in standing, experiment with taking a few slow steps. See what parts of your body get engaged. If you keep your attention on your feet and on the support of the earth, can you release the tension in some of the upper body muscles that habitually get activated when you walk?

- Slowly walk, breathe, and release any unnecessary holding of tension. Feel a new relationship with the earth as you move.

Exercise: Sitting

- Find a firm, flat seated chair and sit without leaning on the chair back. Make sure your feet are firmly on the floor, or use a pillow or low bench for your feet.

- In a way similar to the standing exercise, move your upper torso slightly forward, backwards, to the left and to the right. Find a balance point where you can rely on your hips to support you without strain.

- Enhance the grounded feeling by actually noticing where your body touches the chair and the subtle pressure of the floor against the bottom of each foot. Make sure your abdomen is not constrained by hunching forward too much.

- Close your eyes and feel your feet, noting the subtle ways your feet can add to your experience of support and ease.

- Breathe, allowing your shoulder blades to drop down your back, release your neck, and soften your jaw.

- Explore the possibilities of a new relationship with how your body can use the floor and the chair to feel supported, grounded, open and relaxed.

- Explore ways of changing the position of your computer to allow you the most ease while using it.

If you enjoy these types of learning experiences, consider meeting with practitioners of the Alexander Technique and the Feldenkrais Method who specialize in such awareness training.

Energy Distribution

As a human you have a body that can be seen - muscles, bones, nerves, and organs. You also have a more subtle, unseeable body that is made up of energy channels. Although this subtle body is unseen, it has a powerful influence on how you feel, and it can also be helped or obstructed by your thoughts and movements. Physical practices such as yoga, tai chi and chi gong are formulated to remove obstacles or stuck places in our subtle channels and allow energy to flow freely through the body.

Mind practices such as meditation are also aimed at doing the same thing, through a specific sitting or standing posture and the practice of placing the attention on a specific object. Meditation is a powerful training for balancing your energy and for changing your life. You deliberately "do nothing" for extended periods of time, only to discover a very rich inner world of self-knowledge and a much more perceptive and accurate capability to tune into what is around you. *Practicing* the following exercises can provide a direct experience of freeing your energy.

Exercise: Standing Meditation

One way of combining a physical and mental means of opening your energy channels is standing meditation. It sounds quite easy since you will just be standing in one place, but you may find that it is quite challenging. For this standing meditation start with short sessions (try three minutes) and slowly build up your capacity.

- Find a quiet place where you can stand on a flat supportive surface, either barefoot or in flat shoes. Place your feet about hip width apart. Keep your eyes partially open and look down at the floor. Slightly bend your knees.

- Feel the support of the ground, and find a balance point

where you feel stable (review the previous grounding section). As you stand become as relaxed as you can.

- Count your breaths from 10 down to 1, each in and out breath comprising one unit.

- Then let go of the counting and continue to focus your attention on each breath as you stand. When your mind wanders, bring it back to the sensations of the breath. As you continue to stand, your energy will naturally begin to loosen obstructions to its free flow.

- Pause every few minutes to scan your body for places that are holding tension. Do your best to let the tension go, and then return to breath awareness. Doing this practice daily can be a significant aid in improving your sense of ease and your health.

Exercise: Progressive Muscle Relaxation

When you find yourself waiting, such as when standing in a line or when sitting in a waiting room, you might practice *progressive muscle relaxation*. This involves tensing a part of your body, holding the tension for about 10 seconds, and then releasing it. Starting with your feet, you gradually progress through each part of your body all the way up to and including your face. This is great training in informing the body about when it is

33

unconsciously holding tension, and what it feels like to let it go. This can also be an aid to falling asleep, where you would progressively tense and release each area of your body as you are lying in bed.

This chapter has described many ways of reducing distress. Choose one that appeals to you and focus on it for a week. Make sure you have a way of reminding yourself of your intention, such as marking it in your calendar, setting a reminder in your phone, or putting a note on your desk or refrigerator. At the end of the week either celebrate your success in carrying out your intentions or reflect on ways to do a better job next week.

CHAPTER THREE
PRACTICE CONSCIOUS BENEVOLENCE

Changes in Intention Benefit YOU

I was recently asked to give a talk on stress reduction to a group of very successful business executives. I have been giving stress management presentations for decades, talking about the fight or flight response, about time management and so on, but for this occasion I took a risk and presented a new slant. The main theme became *conscious benevolence for stress management.* It not only made sense to them, it also inspired them to think differently about their approach to themselves, their families and their employees.

The practice of conscious benevolence has had amazingly positive effects on a wide variety of groups with whom I have worked - high powered CEOs, meditation practi-tioners, people struggling with eating disorders, people in individual and group psychotherapy, yoga teachers, physicians and medical students to name a few. Considerable research is being done regarding compassion, and the results show very positive outcomes mentally, physically and socially for people who become more consciously benevolent by practicing compassion meditations and contemplations.

A research paper entitled *Loving-Kindness Meditation practice associated with longer telomeres in women* (Hoge 2013) indicates the profound physical effects of this kind of practice. Telomeres protect the ends of your chromosomes. Shorter telomeres have been linked to chronic stress, and the relatively short length may serve as a marker of accelerated aging. In this research, the telomeres of women who practiced Loving-Kindness Meditation (focusing on unselfish kindness and warmth towards all people) were compared to a control group who did no Loving-Kindness Meditation. The Loving-Kindness Meditation practitioners had *longer* relative telomere lengths (a biomarker associated with longevity) than those in the control group.

Self-Kindness

In moving toward integrating conscious benevolence into your life, applying compassion to yourself in the form of self-kindness is a good place to start. There is a rare truthfulness that accompanies self-kindness. While it is easy to mistake self-kindness for letting yourself off the hook, this is not the case. In fact, self-kindness when practiced properly is the intense generosity of fully being with yourself, as you are. This may sound simple, but having taught self-kindness in workshops for many years, I have found that it is quite a novel notion for most Westerners. By and large we are a self critical and judgmental bunch, coming down on ourselves hard and fast when we miss the mark. In fact, in almost every workshop there are several people reporting that the concept of self-kindness has never even occurred to them, and they marvel at the idea as if discovering a rare gem-stone.

Perhaps you think you won't be motivated if the harsh critic is not on the job. You'll just dissolve into a gooey mass of ineptitude and sloth. But think about it. Are you more likely to take a risk, to try something new if you know you will heap shame and blame on yourself if you fail or alternatively, if you will be extending a friendly hand along with encouragement to pick yourself up and keep going? The research is clear that practicing self-kindness does not reduce feelings of personal responsibility, but actually makes it more likely that you will be able to admit mistakes and move on, cultivating a new sense of resilience in the face of distress.

Researchers Kristen Neff and Roos Vonk found that higher levels of self-compassion have been associated with greater life satisfaction, emotional intelligence, and social connectedness, as well as less self-criticism, depression, anxiety, rumination, thought suppression, perfectionism, and disordered eating behaviors. Besides the psychological benefits, one study on self-compassion noted that it also has a very positive physical effect in that it may serve as a protective factor against stress-induced inflammation and inflammation-related disease (Breines 2014).

Psychologist Kristen Neff is one of the pioneers in self-kindness research and she gives the definition that follows for self-kindness.

SELF-KINDNESS

Being open to and moved by one's own suffering.

Being able to hold painful thoughts and feelings in balanced awareness rather than over identifying with them.

Experiencing feelings of caring and kindness toward oneself in instances of pain or failure rather than being harshly self critical.

Recognizing that one's experience is part of the common human experience.

Aspects of Self-Kindness

There are three key aspects to self-kindness. The first aspect is *a willingness to observe oneself,* in other words practicing mindfulness - present moment awareness of mind and body with a nonjudgmental attitude. This observation is not meant as an opportunity to catch yourself out, but rather is a way of being open to what is really occurring, even when it puts you in a bad light.

You will be guided through learning and practicing mind-fulness throughout this book. Mindfulness and self-kindness compliment each other. It is much more likely you will spend the time in self observation, and also ponder the motivations for your actions if you have been practicing self-kindness/loving-kindness as explained below, and wishing yourself well.

The second aspect of self-kindness is *accommodating or tolerating distress*. This means being able to place an appreciative hand on your own heart and admitting "I am having a hard time." I can't tell you how much this simple act helps. Many people I work with have the habit of feeling distress and immediately trying to escape the discomfort, often by using maladaptive coping strategies such as overeating, drinking alcohol, excessive exercise, workaholism, or drugs. Unfortunately, in the short term, these methods do bring some relief. However, if used consistently they lead to more difficulties than would occur by simply and compassionately recognizing and staying with the original pain.

Accommodating distress means allowing the uncom-fortable feelings to be present. Sometimes we busy ourselves to avoid feeling the vulnerability and sadness that is present in some measure in all of us. Learning to stay present with the experience of that sadness is in fact a strength rather than a weakness. There is a quality of befriending your experience, as it is - noticing the sen-sations in your body and observing the story line. There can be a balanced awareness - not pushing difficult feelings away but also not over identifying with them. Sitting quietly you can note what is going through your mind, be fully present to the direct physical and mental experience, and then let it go - angry thought, craving, sadness, joy - the whole spectrum.

The astute self-knowledge that comes from the first two aspects allows for the third key to self-kindness - *recognizing that being human is messy*. How often do you find yourself knowing what you should do and then not doing it? How often do you say the wrong thing at the wrong time? How often are you stunned by the mess that is your own mind?

Fortunately, the mindfulness/self-kindness practices can help enhance your clarity and self regulation capabilities. Therefore you will be less likely to re-plant the seeds of negative behaviors because you can see these impulses clearly and give yourself enough space to respond positively rather than react habitually.

There are many ways to cultivate self-kindness. It is worth spending time thinking about how you might incorporate the material in the exercises that follow into your life.

Exercise: Self-Kindness Practices

- When you feel emotional distress, instead of immediately focusing on trying to fix the problem, first pause and offer yourself comfort. This could be as simple as stating *I am really suffering right now.* You could also place one hand on your chest as a gesture of comfort. This simple effort enhances your capability for staying with painful moments instead of acting on them (usually without thinking it through), or trying to suppress or escape them. Learning distress tolerance makes it more likely that when you are ready, you will respond to painful situations in a healthier way.

- Notice the tone of voice of your self talk. Can you cultivate a soothing tone of voice and practice supportive language, even if you are acknowledging a part of yourself you dislike?

- Perhaps your behaviors have been poorly thought out and damaging to yourself or others. Attacking yourself makes you feel even worse and is not a great motivator for positive change. Rather than berating yourself for not being "good enough," offer yourself your own friendship, which is especially needed in difficult times. For example you could say *"I can appreciate myself even when I mess up,"* or *"I regret how I behaved and I'm going to support myself in doing better next time."*

This is not the same as letting yourself off the hook, or saying anything goes and is okay. This is a very positive way of *admitting and taking personal responsibility for your actions*, but not destroying yourself in the process. If you are supportive of yourself when you fail, you become less afraid of failing and are more able to take on new challenges. Motivate yourself as you would a friend, providing encouragement and support rather than condemnation.

- Practice wishing yourself well. This means silently repeating to yourself self-kindness phrases. Examples include phrases such as
  May I be well
  May I be peaceful and at ease
  May I hold my suffering in compassion
  May I feel kindness for myself even when I fail
  May I be happy

- Recognize that all people are imperfect, that all people fail at some points in their lives, that all of us make mistakes, and that we have serious life challenges - just as you do.

- Appreciate positive aspects of your life, and frequently express gratitude.

Choose a time each day when you can spend a few moments wishing yourself well. If it feels alien or uncomfortable try simply saying "I want to be a friend to myself."

Exercise: Envisioning

A helpful way of practicing warmth toward yourself is to visualize compassionate images. These images could be of people you admire, spiritual beings, or benevolent animals. Feel the radiance of their compassion, and allow it to soothe the hurting parts of yourself. Using your imagination in this way can change which parts of your brain are engaged - taking energy away from the stress centers and moving it to the positive emotion sections of your brain. This can go a long way in relieving distress and in helping you gain insight into how to resolve difficulties.

Exercise: Practice Conscious Benevolence Toward Yourself in Times of Distress

This exercise is similar to what has been explained above, but puts it in a simple, easy to remember format.

Acknowledge: State to yourself something like *I am having a difficult time,* or *I made a mistake*, or whatever can best describe what you are feeling.

Offer support: *Everyone struggles with these kinds of difficulties. I wish myself comfort and relief from discomfort, emotional distress, difficult circumstances ...*

Use kindness phrases: *May I be well, may I be peaceful and at ease, may I hold my distress in compassion, may I be happy.* Feel free to create your own phrases.

Bring to mind compassionate images: These might be spiritual beings, friends, someone you admire, a pet, or something in nature. Allow yourself to take in the compassion offered by these images.

Whenever I teach these kinds of practices someone always asks if expecting to be at ease, or happy is unrealistic. It is true that suffering is a basic truth about human life, and that everyone will experience painful situations at some time. However, if you take note of this present moment, there is often no reason not to be at ease. Because we tend to worry about the future and fret about the past our mind stays stressed and our body tense.

This is not to say planning and contemplating options for the future, and learning from the past is unimportant. It does point to the fact that often we can't get our mind to stop, even when we are simply sitting in a room. Taking breaks from over conceptualizing in order to have a more balanced perception of the world is what is being referred to here. Most people need some form of mind training to be able to do this, and these compassion practices as well as meditation training are perfect for this purpose.

Exercise: Affectionate Breathing

Sit in a quiet place and focus on your whole body. Relax your shoulders and neck, and then bring your attention to your breath. After a few moments, repeat inwardly to yourself the following phrase for as long as it feels helpful: *Breathing in I take in universal compassion, breathing out I let go of distress.*

If it is difficult for you to feel this in a positive way, stop and simply feel warmth and tenderness for yourself in any way you can, even if it is simply having sympathy for the frustration you feel.

Research by Barbara Fredrickson, PhD showed that people who practiced loving-kindness experienced more positive emotions including love, joy, gratitude, contentment, hope, pride, interest, amusement, and awe. These positive emotions helped people build resources for living successfully. An interesting note about the compassion research is that benefits have occurred for people who did a focused practice over a few months for as brief a time as 15 minutes a day.

Exercise: Loving-Kindness for Others

The following practice is one that you can do either as a contemplation or as an active engagement in the world.

1. It helps to start this practice by warming up your heart in an easily accessible way. Bring to mind someone you feel very good about already. This can be someone you know or someone who is inspiring to you even if you have never met them. Imagine their presence and in your mind, simply wish them well. This can be by using the phrase *May you be well,* or with any phrase that suits you. Other examples include *May you feel peace, May you be happy,* or *May you be safe.* The point is to be able to easily awaken your heart, your compassion and to engage the positive emotions part of your brain.

2. When you feel ready you can bring in other friends and relatives you feel good about and mentally wish them well.

3. If you would like to broaden your connections, bring to mind people you usually overlook, who you feel neutral about but who are part of your everyday life - the office cleaner, mail person, grocery bagger and so on. Wish them well.

4. After you have practiced in this way a number of times, consider bringing to mind someone you are not that fond of, who irritates you, and notice what happens if you also wish them well. Over time, notice what may be changing. Does it change your own physiology in a positive way? Does it change your attitude toward them? Are you able to have more choice regarding whether you feel irritated by them or not?

5. Imagine sending your good wishes and heart felt warmth to all beings. Feel the radiance of those good wishes spreading throughout the world.

Doing these kindness practices for a few minutes a day can have very powerful positive effects on your own mental and physical wellbeing. You can practice formally when sitting in a quiet place, and also engage as you go about your day by wishing people well when you are driving, in the office, or at the store. Over time you can deepen your capabilities for befriending yourself and caring about others.

CHAPTER FOUR

TAME OVERCONSUMPTION

How many times have you had the experience of standing in the dark kitchen, your puzzled face illuminated by the light coming out of the open refrigerator? All you know is that you want something, and there is hope you will find it in the leftover chocolate cake sitting on the shelf. This haunted search is familiar to most of us because we live compelled by desire.

We hunger, we experience a fundamental and pervasive dissatisfaction with what is, and expend enormous amounts of time and energy in striving to attain a better external circumstance and a more satisfying state of mind. Please note that what is being referred to here is *unhealthy desire*, desire that hooks you, that tends to keep your mind stirred up, and that gives rise to greed, possessiveness, and excessive consumption. *Healthy desire,* on the other hand, is that which propels you toward fulfilling a deeper internal mission, and tends to give rise to happiness and generosity.

As you have probably recognized, reducing unhealthy desires, the persistent hunger, the craving is not easy. Much of our mental energy is focused on getting what we want, and we live in a consumer based society that reinforces these constant urges toward eating or drinking too much, buying the latest clothing style, furniture, car etc., things that tend to provide only temporary satisfaction. Fortunately it is possible to train yourself in recognizing, loosening, and eventually liberating yourself from this persistent craving and grasping that leads to overconsumption.

Overcoming Craving

There are three components to overcoming the craving that leads to excessive consumption. The first is examining the "wanting mind" itself, the second is becoming more savvy about how your attention gets fixated on what you want, and the third is learning how to transform this fixation into an offering.

Examining the Wanting Mind

"Wanting" is a universal phenomenon, and our mental list of what we want is seemingly endless. We wake up in the morning and ask "What do I want today? What do I want to eat, what do I want to buy, how much do I want?" Wanting, when it goes beyond our basic, ordinary needs, is an expression of a longing for something either more than or different from what we already have. There is a sense of being fundamentally unfulfilled. It is well worth looking more deeply into the nature of wanting, recognizing how you know wanting is there, and *naming* it. When you become familiar with recognizing and naming wanting, then it will become easier to notice when you are captured, and therefore more likely you will be able to free yourself. You can also get more specific about the elements of wanting or craving by naming what sense is activated and what it is seeking. For example, craving is arising through seeing – seeing a form I want, or craving is arising through tasting – wanting pleasure from tongue contact. You may even notice a craving for ideas, for mental stimulation.

With practice you can become better at noticing the "I want" state of mind, let it arise, look at it, and let it go. By observing desire itself and by letting it go again and again, you can bring a more settled and satisfying sense of *equanimity* into your life, instead of being constantly subject to a never ending series of desires.

Loosening Fixation
The second component in diminishing craving is to notice when your attention has become fixated. A fixation is a narrowing of attention onto one thing that we are strongly attracted to or repelled by. If it is attraction, a very compelling momentum is created to get the object of fixation, including having thoughts about the object as well as feeling a physical sensation, something like a hole that needs to be filled.

Having a fixation also includes the tendency of the mind to embellish the desirable qualities of what you want, while ignoring the "downside," the undesirable aspects or the future consequences. Food is one of the more common ways we fixate and ignore future consequences. The reward centers of the brain light up and leave your good intentions regarding health and weight in the dark. Or, when you see an article of clothing you desire your imagination revels in how nice it would be to possess it, and all promises regarding budget, savings, and other necessities get forgotten.

You can separate wanting from getting by using conscious awareness to break your fixation of attention. Imagine your child is being carried out to sea by a strong undertow. You would not try to fight with the undertow (the object) but would grab your child (your attention) and pull her back to shore.

If you practice becoming more aware of your attention as an aspect of your mind that you can actually take charge of and use as a support, you can notice when it has been kidnapped and deliberately take it back. Learning the Awareness of Breath meditation practices that follow in Chapter 5 provide a very good method for training your attention not to wander. When you notice your mind has gone astray, has been "carried out to sea," you simply bring it back to the neutral object of attention, in this case the breath.

Making Offerings
Another way of loosening fixation is to offer the object of your desire. I have made it a practice to leave a small portion of food on my plate and I mentally offer it at the end of the meal, saying something like "May all beings have enough to eat." I've noticed that this has several results. First, it reduces my speedy and mindless eating

tendencies. Second, it makes every meal feel like a shared universal experience. Additionally, when I actually offer the food I feel a warmth in my heart, a momentary radiance of compassion that both softens and uplifts my own state of mind. By starting with our own mind, we can begin to reverse the craving that often drives our behaviors.

Exercise: Make Offerings

You can do an offering practice with anything that has aroused your craving state of mind.

- With food, setting aside a small portion before eating as an offering will slow the speed and interrupt the habitual patterns that often drive overeating. Offering this portion of food at the end of the meal by placing it outside can signal that you are finished eating, and prevent mindlessly continuing.

- When you notice craving arise while shopping, you might wish that all beings have the warmth and comfort of the cashmere sweater you crave, and actually open your hand in a gesture of offering it to them.

- Take an offering walk through a mall. Whenever you notice your mind is captured by desire release that state of mind by mentally offering what you want to others.

These offering gestures can cause an shift in brain activity from a narrow "me" focus to a more connected and empathic part of the brain. Test this for yourself. Most people feel happier when released from the "I want" state of mind into the more open hearted feelings arising from kindness and generosity.

Direct Experience
The next time you find yourself "standing at the refrigerator door," stop and notice. What am I doing here? What do I feel in my chest, my heart? Can I give it a name? Recognize your attention has gone in search of an object for your wanting, has fixated on something external to try to quell the pain of your longing and dissatisfaction. Bring your attention back to simply being present with what you are experiencing. Sit down for a moment and hold that feeling in compassion. Be fully present with this wanting, as it is, with an open heart. Perhaps put a comforting hand on your chest. Then you can offer whatever you are struggling with by saying something like "May everyone have the food they need, the happiness they seek, and may they attain relief from the suffering of a dissatisfied mind."

Freeing yourself from grasping can actually increase the pleasure you can experience from the objects around you, whether you own them or not. You can recognize attraction itself, and relax into it as an experience of appreciation rather than of wanting. The object is all the more precious if it is then let go, freeing you to continue experiencing your world without getting stuck. Attraction is not a problem, trying to glue yourself to the object of your attraction is where the pain arises.

Summary
In summary, the steps to reduce craving and thereby lead a more satisfying life are to 1) recognize the wanting mind, 2) relax attentional fixation, and 3) psychologically and/or physically offer the object of your desire. As individuals we have the opportunity to redirect the momentum of wanting into one of generosity and caring. This will go a long way toward transforming our mind and relieving the intense dissatisfaction that drives our craving.

Portions of this chapter were originally published in the Shambhala Sun magazine, July 2011.

CHAPTER FIVE

TAKE BRAIN BREAKS

In general, we take our brain for granted. Most of us go about our day without much thought about how to take care of this most precious resource. This chapter will guide you through a number of methods for becoming more conscious of ways to make sure your brain is working at its optimal level.

Ultradian Rhythms

One of the executives I was counseling regarding stress management stated that in general his method was to "power through" whatever stress he was under, apparently with little regard for the effects on his body or mental wellbeing. This may work for a while, especially if you have the physiological reserves of youth. However, if you consider that, on average, we lose about one percent of organ function per year after the age of 25, powering through might eventually backfire. Think about your work style. When your energy is starting to flag what do you do - just keep going, get another cup of coffee, look for a sugar fix?

As human beings we are subject to natural cycles or rhythms. We are all familiar with the circadian rhythm of night and day. Another cycle you may not be aware of is what is called ultradian rhythms. This is a shorter cycle that happens within the context of the larger day and night cycle. In general, every 90 minutes your energy goes through a cycle of rising and falling. We are built to expend energy and then rest, so we can renew our energy rather than using up all of our reserves, leaving us exhausted. Instead of trying to keep your energy up consistently through your work day, deliberately taking brain breaks when you feel the 90 minute slump can renew your thinking capabilities in a natural way, and most likely improve your work performance.

Brain Integration

In our ordinary daily experience, we are generally not consciously integrating our right and left brain hemispheres. There is evidence from a study headed by Petr Bob, PhD entitled *Conscious attention, meditation, and bilateral information transfer* that we can do a better job of integrating information from our various brain regions with training in meditation practices such as the ones that follow. Another study noted that yoga techniques that included physical postures, breathing exercises and meditation may be associated with the promotion of beneficial neuroplastic changes in executive brain systems (Froeliger 2012).

Meditation

Meditation is a proven method for reducing stress. One particular method is the Awareness of Breath meditation, which is an ancient technique that is central to most meditation traditions. It is also an important part of the Mindfulness-Based Stress Reduction (MBSR) program that has received international recognition for the benefit it offers. This is an eight week training that has been the subject of hundreds of research studies showing its benefit for a wide range of mental and physical ailments. A recent study also found significant decreases in primary and specialty care visits and for Emergency Department visits and hospital admissions as a result of participation in the MBSR program (McCubbin 2014). I have taught this program as part of both the Duke Integrative Medicine and the University of North Carolina Integrative Medicine Programs and can attest to its value.

A simple way to learn the Awareness of Breath technique is by using breath counting. A recent study noted that skill in breath counting was associated with more meta-awareness, less mind wandering, better mood, and greater non-attachment (Levinson 2014). Meta-awareness is the capacity to notice that a mental experience is happening - a thought, sensation, or the mind wandering away from the task at hand. The greater non-attachment that results from the practice of Awareness of Breath through breath counting is also worth noting here, since it means that you are less likely to be captured by distractions formerly paired with reward. In other words, you can resist eating too much and other negative behaviors that usually stimulate your brain's reward center but lead to unhealthy results. You are better able to consciously choose the object of your attention and to let go of unhealthy impulses.

Exercise: Breath Counting Meditation

For this meditation, I suggest you start with practicing for five minutes, and gradually build up to twenty minutes. Find a quiet place where you won't be disturbed (away from electronics) and sit either in a chair or on a meditation cushion on the floor. Having an upright posture is important for both staying alert and for a free flow of breath. You can do this practice with your eyes closed or with them open with a soft gaze directed at the floor. In addition to enhancing your attentional capabilities, remember that this is also a form of practicing self-kindness.

- Begin by spending a moment simply noticing your breath.

- Then start counting your breath. A combination of the in and the out breath counts as one. It is helpful to say the number silently to yourself in the space between the in and out breath so you can also be present for the direct experience of the flow of each breath. I'd like to emphasize this point. Counting is the technique for allowing you to stay present enough to experience each breath. The direct experience of each breath is the important part of the meditation.

- Attempt to count up to 10, maintaining your attention on each breath. When you lose track of where you are, which is very likely in the beginning, simply start again. This is a good moment to practice being non-judgmental toward yourself. When you catch the inner critic making a comment, just let it go and come back to the breath awareness. Remember that learning a new skill takes time and effort.

- When you are able to maintain your attention all the way to counting ten breaths, start over with one after reaching the tenth breath and keep going.

- You can keep track of the time by setting a timing app on your phone that has a gentle signal such as a chime (and then putting it in hearing range but out of sight), or by looking at a clock now and again. If you commit to a certain number of minutes it is important that you stay and practice for that amount of time. It is good training in keeping your word to yourself, and it helps the mind strengthen its capability to stay on task.

- When the time is up, spend a moment noticing your body and state of mind. Even if you have had difficulty keeping track of the counting you may notice a positive effect. Appreciate yourself for your efforts. Then rise and go about your day, knowing that you can come back to this practice at any time. Even practicing for a minute in the midst of stress can be beneficial.

After doing this practice consistently for several weeks you may find that at times your mind naturally settles. When this happens you can let go of counting for as long as that naturally settled, alert but relaxed mind state lasts. Then, if your mind drifts off or gets captured by a story line, start counting again to renew your attentiveness.

Going Further
In this book I will describe a number of mindfulness and meditation techniques. I have been studying and practicing meditation for many years and have included in this book methods that are most easily usable. However, if meditation interests you, I strongly encourage you to seek an experienced meditation teacher and receive personal instruction from them as well as guidance in your practice. Regarding yoga, there are many books, websites and reasonably accessible classes for learning yoga. I suggest you look for a teacher that offers breathing exercises and meditation as an integral part of each class. Solely doing postures leaves out the most important parts of reconnecting mind and body in a healthy way.

Sensory awareness
If you think about it, it makes sense that if you are using one section of the brain in a concentrated way as you work, it is likely to get fatigued. Focusing on one of your senses for a few minutes can relieve the cognizing part of your brain. Shifting focus could mean stopping to listen to bird sounds outside, taking a music listening break, or

just deliberately tuning in, in a relaxed way, to the sounds occurring wherever you are. A sensory break might also be massaging your hands or feet, or stretching your body.

If your work entails closely focusing on reading or computer work, go outside and look up at the sky. Rest your gaze there, feeling the expansiveness of the space around you. If you are lucky enough to work close to a natural setting, go outside and use your sense of smell. When you need a snack, instead of eating it while you work, sit quietly and be deliberate about tasting each bite.

All of these sensory endeavors will allow the fatigued part of your brain to renew itself as you switch your attention to activities that stimulate a different part of your brain. A benefit of sensory awareness is that it automatically brings you into the present moment. It takes you out of the brain regions concerned with the past and the future and allows for being more freely present in each moment. There are additional sensory awareness practices in Chapter 6.

Power nap
When you hit the fatigue part of your energy cycle actually taking a short nap is a great idea. A ten minute nap can refresh you without leading to the fogginess of longer sleep. A ten minute nap is also less likely to cause you the difficulty in falling asleep at night that longer naps do. Set your phone to chime or make some other non-jarring sound to wake you in ten minutes. If you have a private office, bring a beach towel or yoga mat to

work and lie down on the floor to rest both your body and your mind.

Contemplation

It is normal when concentrating on something to narrow your focus to a small area of your life. When it is time to take a break and refresh your brain, consider keeping short passages nearby from books that inspire you and allow you to recall the bigger picture. In a relaxed way, spend a few moments recalling the deeper meaning of your life by contemplating these passages.

A traditional way of practicing contemplation is to sit in a quiet place and either read a specific phrase or bring to mind a particular topic. Occasionally bring the topic or phrase to mind, and in between just rest quietly or do an Awareness of Breath meditation practice. This will allow you to access parts of your consciousness that are beyond mere intellect and thereby provide more creative and meaningful insights. Contemplations could include questions such as the following:

- What is meaningful about this day?
- What qualities do I admire in others?
- What does equanimity mean to me?

Media Relief

Studies have shown that watching or listening to excessive news coverage can induce a stress response. After the Boston Marathon bombing, repeated media exposure (six or more hours) regarding the event was associated with higher acute stress than was experienced by those who were actually there (Holman 2013).

It is natural for your attention to be captured by traumatic events, but it is worth looking closely at your own responses and actively turn off whatever media coverage you are attending to. It is very easy to be listening to the radio during breakfast and hear about hundreds of people being killed in various ways all over the world. This has an effect on your body and mental state that is most likely not positive.

How much news do you need in a day? Would you consider limiting the time you spend watching the latest tragedies, war updates, local violence and disturbing incidences that fear journalism thrives on? It does capture your attention, but a steady diet of such things skews your view of the world, and provokes negative mental and physical reactions to all sorts of world activity over which you have no control.

You may have the habit of automatically turning on the radio, computer or TV as background noise, but it is still having an effect, even though you may not be consciously aware of it. Try experimenting with more silence, or with carefully chosen media that will enhance your day rather than contribute to your unease.

This chapter has guided you through a number of ways to bring relief to your brain. I'd like to emphasize the

Awareness of Breath meditation practice, as this can be a lifelong aid in not only bringing daily relief, but also in deepening your capability to enhance your own mind/ body health.   It may not be an easy practice in the beginning, but most people gain appreciation for its effects the longer they stay with it.

CHAPTER SIX

RESET YOUR INTERNAL COMPASS

The Problem of Me

Much of our distress arises out of the habitual way we get very focused on ourselves, seeing the world solely in terms of how it effects *me*. This consumes a lot of energy unnecessarily and tends to keep you going around in mental circles when you could be relaxing and enjoying yourself instead. An easy way of remedying this tendency is to focus on something outside of yourself. This could be done by simply looking up at the sky and feeling the vastness, by contemplating how others might be effected by the situation, by practicing conscious benevolence, or by engaging more of a sensory connection to the world.

Gain a Broader Perspective

When you are feeling painfully self involved and want to broaden your perspective try the following. Bring to mind an interactive difficulty you are experiencing - family discord, a work conflict or a neighborhood problem, for example. We tend to focus on ourselves as the central character and act accordingly. As an alternative, imagine someone you feel neutral about in your place. What changes? If the situation was happening to them, what would you do about it? Can you see some alternatives that might not have occurred to you when you are not in the center? Is it easier to understand the perspective of the other people involved? It can be very helpful to all concerned to occasionally step back from a situation in this way and reassess your view.

Compassion

Another way of becoming less self involved is through practicing compassion. Researcher Richard Davidson used functional magnetic resonance imaging to measure what parts of the brain were activated when people did compassion meditation. It showed activity in the positive emotions regions and also reduced activity in the areas that kept track of what is self and what is other (Goleman 2003). When you are engaging in benevolent activity or contemplations, the "selfing" part of the brain gets quiet, and you feel more connected to the world in a positive way. Review the chapter on conscious benevolence to become more compassionately engaged.

Sensory Awareness

There have been several sensory awareness exercises in previous chapters. The ones in this chapter have a different focus and can help you learn to use your senses to shift out of the "selfing" sections of your brain and provide a broader sense of connection with the world. They appear to be simple, but may take some investment of time in practicing to be able to develop a new skill and to remember you have another option to your usual stance in the world. Doing brief sessions - a few minutes at a time - works best. It will help you *reset your psychological compass* by allowing you to connect with the outer world in new ways.

Exercise: Hearing

Even though our ears are always working, we are not often *consciously* hearing. Adding the conscious element to hearing can take you out of the stress centers of your brain very quickly, and bring a sense of ease. To begin your training in sensory awareness, go outside and sit or stand somewhere where you feel safe and comfortable. You can do this exercise with your eyes open or closed, whichever way makes it easiest for you to focus your attention on hearing.

Spend the next five minutes or so simply tuning in to the sounds around you. If you notice yourself naming everything, see if you can let that go and just simply hear in a very relaxed way. When you notice your mind drifting off into a train of thinking, gently bring it back to this deep sense of listening, of being wholly present in this moment of sound. Gradually, as you practice this, you can develop a capability for less commentary and more non-conceptual presence.

Exercise: Seeing

Our normal way of seeing has a sense of our eyes looking outward and subtly grasping at the external world. In this practice of seeing, relax your body and eyes enough to allow sights to come to you in a very effortless manner. To practice this, sit in a quiet place and relax your body as much as possible. With your eyes open, soften your gaze so that you are not looking at anything in particular, and allow your eyes to perceive in a very effortless, general way.

In the same way as you did with hearing, when you notice your mind trying to busy itself naming everything, let that go and relax more deeply into being present and open to the world in front of you, as it is. Practicing non-grasping in this way allows the world to come to you, and can be beautifully relaxing.

Exercise: Smelling

The pleasure that can be derived from smelling often goes unnoticed. Have you ever inhaled near the opening of a bag of freshly ground coffee? If you like coffee, this can be a heavenly experience. A large part of enjoying a meal has to do with smell, and you can enhance the pleasure and relaxing aspects of eating if you consciously focus on the scents of your food. It also helps you to be present for the experience, and consequently feel satisfied with appropriate amounts of food.

Consciously noticing the smells in nature, the multi-faceted scents in the forest or by the shore, is like getting an aromatherapy session for free. Take yourself out for an aroma walk and notice the results.

Exercise: Tasting

We each have our favorite tastes, and seek ways of satisfying our urges to get salty, sweet, sour or bitter tastes. The first few bites are an opportunity get the most pleasure out of your food, because your taste buds are fresh and have not been dulled to a particular taste. However, we often miss this opportunity because we are not paying attention. Choose a specific food you like and really attend, without distraction, to the first few bites. Feel the texture and savor the taste. You might set an intention to develop the habit of pausing to really taste your meal at frequent intervals.

Exercise: Touching

We are always touching something - our feet on the floor, body in a chair or bed, hand on a door knob and so on. It is so common that we rarely notice the sensation of touch. Stop and notice the ways your body is in touch with the world. Spend time focusing on the exquisite sensitivity of your hands as you use them throughout the day.

Healing Chi Gong

I have spent several years studying and practicing Healing Chi Gong and find it quite effective. This is a way of training originating in Asia that focuses on understanding and influencing the subtle energy channels of the body in a way that supports health. After you practice for some time, you may begin to realize that *energy follows attention.* Recognizing this, you can become more adept at using your mind to guide energy to areas of your body that need help.

One exercise that is common to most Chi Gong teaching lineages is called either the Microcosmic Orbit or the Small Universe. It involves bringing your attention through particular points on the surface of your body in a way that smooths out and regenerates your energy. It is similar to the way acupuncture points work. As has been mentioned in previous exercises, it is more important to be gentle with yourself than to get it just right. Being relaxed and engaged will be the most helpful way of practicing this exercise.

Exercise: Refocus Energy with the Microcosmic Orbit

- Begin by touching the tip of your tongue to the roof of your mouth behind your front teeth, and let it stay there throughout this exercise.

- Bring your attention to your abdomen, an inch or two below your navel. Imagine a small circle of light there, half in and half out of the surface of your body. Breathe in and out as this ball of light rests there.

- Then imagine that ball of light slowly traveling along your body's surface until it gets to your perineum at the base of your torso. Again, as you rest your attention there, pause for one in and out breath.

- The next point is the tip of your tailbone, and while envisioning the light there take one in and out breath.

- Continue circling around your body in this way, pausing for a breath
    -at the point on your back opposite your navel,

-the point at the base of your skull,
-then bring the ball of light around the top of
   your head to the point between your eyebrows,
-to the front of your throat,
-the middle of your chest and
-back to the original point below your navel.

- Keep going in this way for a few minutes, down the front of your body and up the back of your body.

- When you are ready to end the practice feel your energy gathering into a ball of light at the point below your navel. Bring that ball into the center of your body and let it stay there, energizing you through the day.

The next time you find yourself obsessing about something, be more active in resetting your internal compass. Let other parts of your brain become engaged, making it much more likely you will be at ease and your insight and wisdom will get an opportunity to be heard and be of help.

CHAPTER SEVEN

USE THE PLACEBO EFFECT

The Placebo Effect

A placebo is a product or action that in one context would have no effect but in another may actually result in physiological changes as well as mental relief. You have probably heard of studies where patients were given a placebo treatment (pills with no active ingredients for example) which resulted in improvement in their medical condition - a placebo effect. These effects can range from changes in blood pressure, heart rate, pain levels, and even reductions in anxiety and depression.

I had an experience that proved the point regarding the placebo effect on pain control. I had a bad headache and went and got an Advil tablet. In about 20 minutes my headache subsided. The next day I found the Advil tablet on the counter where apparently I had left it, never actually having taken it - but believing that I did. When you believe something relieves pain, your body releases endorphins that do so.

One study reported in 2010 had some very interesting results. A team of researchers led by Dr. Ted Kaptchuk compared two groups of people who suffered from Irritable Bowel Syndrome (IBS), a chronic condition accompanied by pain and constipation. One group did not receive any treatment. The other patients were actually told they would be taking fake drugs with no active ingredients, which came in bottles labeled "placebo pills" and told also that placebos often have healing effects.

The results of the study surprised even the investigators themselves. Patients who knew they were taking placebos - the so called fake drugs - described actual improvement, reporting twice as much symptom relief as the no-treatment group. According to Dr. Kaptchuk that is comparable to the improvements seen in trials for the best real IBS drugs.

Further interesting research was done by Dr. Kaptchuk in collaboration with gastro-enterologists in 2008. In this experiment adults with IBS were divided into three groups: a no-treatment control group, told they were on a waiting list for treatment; a second group who received sham acupuncture with minimal interaction with the practitioner; and a third group who received sham acupuncture along with a lot of personal attention - a minimum of 20 minutes of interaction. The interviewer for the sham acupuncture/personal attention group incorporated at least five primary behaviors including: a warm, friendly manner; active listening (such as repeating patient's words, asking for clarifications); empathy (such as saying "I can understand how difficult

IBS must be for you"); 20 seconds of thoughtful silence while feeling the pulse or pondering the treatment plan; and communication of confidence and positive expectation. Practitioners were also required to touch the hands or shoulders of members of the third group. The results showed that the patients who experienced the greatest relief were the third group - those who received the most interactive care.

It is very important that when you are selecting your health care providers that you choose professionals who are kind, comforting, who listen and who believe in and are encouraging about your capacity to heal. The interaction itself can be a very powerful healing encounter.

Another study on exercise, mindset, and the placebo effect is quite interesting. In this study, 84 female hotel room cleaners were measured on health variables affected by exercise. One group was told that the work they did (cleaning the rooms) was good exercise and satisfied the Surgeon General's recommendations for an active lifestyle. They were given examples of how their work qualified as exercise. The women in the control group were not given this information, but they did the same work.

Although the actual behavior of the room cleaners did not change, a month after the intervention the informed group perceived themselves to be getting significantly more exercise than before. "As a result, compared with the control group, they showed a decrease in weight, blood pressure, body fat, waist-to-hip ratio, and body mass index." These results, say the researchers Alia Crum and Ellen Langer, "support the hypothesis that exercise affects health in part or in whole via the placebo effect."

The results described in these placebo effect studies are mind boggling. We are pretty familiar with the ways our mind can produce a negative physical effect, but apparently, the way we think and conceptualize our activities can have a more positive effect than we might ordinarily imagine. It would be worth getting creative about ways you could take advantage of these effects. Note that these activities are not the same as affirmations, where you try to convince yourself of something by repeating positive phrases. Here you are actually doing something to benefit yourself, but how you conceptualize it can boost its power. A few possibilities include the following:

- When you take a medication, imagine the healing effect you seek is taking place.

- When you eat healthy foods, envision yourself as more energetic.

- Research any chronic condition that afflicts you and envision ways your body can turn it around and return to full functioning.

Using Imagery for Healing

Most people have had the experience of making themselves ill by having stressful thoughts - and the link between stress and disease is well documented. The new field of psycho-neuroimmunology examines how your mind/thoughts and your immune system interact. The images you create in your mind are very powerful in creating physiological changes in your body. For example, if you imagine tasting a lemon, your saliva probably increases. If you imagine you are on a beach, lying in the warm sunlight, hearing the soft murmur of waves coming to shore, you start relaxing and your blood flow changes in a positive way. This is very similar to a placebo effect - if your mind believes something is happening it reacts and sends signals to your body as if it *is* actually occurring.

In an article entitled *The Effects of Guided Imagery on the Immune System: a critical review* (Trakhtenberg 2008) it was noted that guided imagery "can reduce stress and elevate the immune system; cell-specific imagery can effect corresponding white blood cells, neutrophils, or lymphocytes." These cells are mediators of immunity that are responsible for collecting and taking away foreign matter. In other words, if you are stressed and spend time imagining yourself walking through a lovely park on a warm day, it can actually reverse your stress response. If you are ill and you imagine your white blood cells increasing and overtaking the illness, there can be a measurable increase in your white blood cell count.

Exercise: Immune Enhancement Imagery

When my mother, at an advanced age, was suffering from pneumonia, she reported using an image of a deer roaming about in her lungs and eating all the cells that were causing her illness. She did very well regarding recovery. You can be very creative regarding the images you use. Images that enhance relaxation and encourage the resources you already have are particularly effective.

What kinds of images represent enhancing the immune system for you? It could be something as simple as smiling at your white blood cells as they go about their work, or it could be imagining the immune cells attracting light to help them brighten up the cells not doing very well. Relax and have fun in imagining positive changes in your body.

Using Memory for Healing

If you are struggling with an illness or chronic health condition, can you remember a time in your life when you felt healthy, when you could run and play, or hike, or ride a bicycle? Remembering a past state of wellness can help your body re-awaken it's innate healing capabilities. Herbert Benson, a physician and researcher who has spent his career studying mind/body methods for healing calls this process *remembered wellness.* Pairing a relaxed state with memories of times in your life when you felt good and felt vibrant health can be very beneficial. Envision as many details as possible in recalling past healthy and energetic states, reliving the joy of activity and movement.

The information in this chapter is meant to help you use the power of your own mind in addition to the advice of your health practitioners to benefit your healing process. Your body has miraculous capabilities that you can access by using a new focus. Be creative in finding novel ways to use the placebo effect for your benefit.

CHAPTER EIGHT
CARE FOR YOUR BODY

Nourish Yourself
Many people I have worked with experience a daily struggle regarding their relationship with food. Either they eat too much and are in an unhealthy weight range, or their weight is in a healthy range but they are conflicted about every bite of food eaten. I have spent many years counseling people with disordered eating, including several years providing group and individual psychotherapy at Duke Diet and Fitness Center and Duke Integrative Medicine. In the context of this book I am focusing on several simple ways to have the most impact on achieving and maintaining a healthy eating style. For a more thorough engagement in the topic you can read my book - *Eating with Fierce Kindness: A Mindful and Compassionate Guide to Losing Weight.*

Mindfulness
Mindfulness is all about paying attention in a new way. Most of us often find ourselves thinking of something else while we go about the activities of our day, and are rarely fully in the present moment. Mindfulness means

paying closer attention to our activities of everyday life - washing the dishes, eating, walking, speaking, and so on, and it also includes the more formal practice of meditation. You have learned about meditation in other chapters where mindfulness of breath, body, and mind is the aim. In this section we are focusing on learning mindfulness skills for everyday life - paying attention in the present moment to whatever is occurring.

In the book *Mindless Eating* author and researcher Brian Wansick describes an astonishing range of ways we fool ourselves about how much we are eating. He notes that simple, usually unnoticed things like the shape of a glass or the size of a plate have a big influence on portion perception. And, we tend to persistently underestimate how much we are eating.

To counter this tendency to fool ourselves regarding food amounts, take the following phrase to heart: *In order to change, first you have to know what you are currently doing.* The two exercises that follow will help you clearly see your unhelpful habits regarding food and eating as well as ways you are making positive choices. In doing these exercises you are more likely to be successful if you see it as an aspect of self care rather than a method of criticizing yourself. Imagine that you are the scientist investigating your own thoughts and behaviors to see what is helpful and what can be let go.

Exercise: Keep Track

Keeping track has proven to be one of the top ways of being successful in clearly recognizing how much you are eating and where the problem areas are. For three days keep track of everything you eat by writing it down right after eating it. Write down everything, no matter how small or seemingly insignificant. This means you need to either write it in your phone or in a small notebook you carry with you. If you would like to do the advanced form of this exercise also write down the time of day and why you are eating. This exercise can be beneficial if you are eating too much and also if you are not eating enough, or if you are starving yourself and then losing control and bingeing.

At the end of the three days look back at your notes to see if there are any patterns, and reflect on what triggers non-hunger eating, or what triggers being overly restrictive in how much you eat. Choose a place where you would like to make a change and plan how you will implement it. Focusing on one manageable change at a time will help you be successful.

Continuing

For those of you who are trying to lose weight, many of the people who have lost weight and are successful in maintaining that weight loss continue to keep track in some way that suits their needs. For example, weighing their portions once a month or using a calorie counting app as a reality check, or keeping a food diary like the one suggested here. Our brains have a way of distorting what we are actually doing and need an accurate reference point now and again. It is also helpful to think through your home in terms of food access. Make healthy foods more accessible and make access difficult for less healthy foods or foods for special occasions.

Mindful Eating

Mindful eating is a way of engaging your attention and all of your senses when you eat. I have often noticed that people who say they love food are actually paying very little attention when they eat. As a result, it is more difficult to notice when you have had a satisfying amount, or when you have had enough of the pleasure of certain tastes. This inattention can then lead to over-eating.

Exercise: Mindful Eating

What follows are suggestions for paying attention to eating in a new way. Choose a day when you have no social engagements. For a whole day follow these guidelines any time you are eating:

• Do not start eating until you are sitting down and relaxed. This in itself could be quite life changing.

Appreciate the fact that you are going to nourish yourself.

- Notice your food - the colors and aromas. Assuming you are going to eat something you like, this adds to your satisfaction and also to your memory of having eaten (curbing the tendency to seek more food later).

- Eat the first three bites very slowly, really noticing the tastes and textures. Your taste buds are most alert at the beginning and you can really savor the tastes you seek - salty, sweet, sour, bitter.

- Eat the rest of your meal at a pace where you can continue to pay attention in a relaxed way. Stay present with whatever bite of food is in your mouth rather than preparing the next bite. Putting your utensils down after each bite helps break the habit of speed and inattention. Notice when your level of hunger diminishes and you begin getting full. Investigate how you make the decision regarding when to stop eating.

- When you are finished, create a signal for yourself that indicates the meal is over (to keep from picking at any food left on your plate). This may be something like saying a gratitude phrase, pushing your plate away, or putting your napkin over the plate.

- At the end of the day consider what effect mindfulness had on your eating habits. Which aspects of mindful eating would you like to incorporate into your daily life? Even something as simple as taking a few relaxing breaths before starting to eat, and really tasting the first few bites can be very helpful.

Reconsider Your Sugar Intake

Sugar, in its many forms, is now pervasive in our processed food and our restaurant food. There is good evidence that sugar has addictive qualities, as noted in articles such as one entitled *Evidence that intermittent, excessive sugar intake causes endogenous opioid dependence* (Colantuoni 2002). One researcher remarks that "in most mammals, including rats and humans, sweet receptors evolved in ancestral environments poor in sugars and are thus not adapted to high concentrations of sweet tastants ....which would generate a supranormal reward signal in the brain with the potential to override self-control mechanisms and thus lead to addiction" (Lenoir 2007). In other words, your brain is not equipped to handle the highly concentrated sweetness of sugar, and the reward section of your brain gets triggered into wanting more and more.

There is also a link between stress and excessive sugar intake. A study by Dr. Daryl O'Connor (2008) showed that stress causes people to choose unhealthy high-fat and high-sugar snacks in preference to healthier food choices. Also, people under stress tend to eat less than usual in their main meals, including their vegetable intake, but shift their preference to high-fat/high-sugar snacks instead. If that isn't bad enough, there is new evidence that sugar also contributes to high blood pressure (Jalal 2010), and sadly, that consumption of sugar and sugar-sweetened foods increases the risk of pancreatic cancer (Larsson 2006).

So, here we are again with the outdated brain problem. Sugar is an intense substance, not found in nature in its current highly processed form, and the reward centers in our brains get completely captured, resulting in craving and withdrawal symptoms - in other words, addiction. Personally, I spent many months reducing my sugar intake, and now ordinary desserts taste excessively sweet and have become much less appealing. I also don't want to spend my time strategizing about how to get my next sugar fix. The natural sweetness found in fruits has become much more appealing. You might think about sugar as if it were a spice. You would never put a cup of any spice in your food, but an occasional sprinkle adds a bit of interest. For optimal success in making diet changes, make sure you are also reducing your stress levels by following the guidance and doing the exercises in this book.

Eat Breakfast

There are many reasons to skip breakfast - you are in a rush, you think it could help you lose weight, or you don't feel like fixing it before going to work. It is understandable but counterproductive. Habits such as skipping meals have been associated with weight gain, dyslipidemia, insulin sensitivity and diabetes mellitus. Studies showed that men who did not eat breakfast had a

33% higher risk of coronary heart disease as compared to men who did eat breakfast (Cahill 2013).

Not eating for a long stretch of time (overnight and well into the next day) creates a starving/overeating cycle that is unhealthy. Simple ways of insuring you get breakfast could include carrying packets of unsweetened instant oatmeal - where you just need to add hot water, or mixtures of nuts and seeds (walnuts and sunflower and pumpkin seeds for example).

Sleep

Through the many years I have consulted with people I have noticed that the complaints about not sleeping have risen dramatically. Perhaps the increased difficulty sleeping and the rise in the number of cell towers and in the use of electronic devices is not coincidental. One of the common recommendations regarding better sleep is to stop using any electronic devices at least an hour before bedtime, and to keep them out of your bedroom.

There are many whole books written about getting a better night's sleep, so I will not go into great detail here. Besides creating a routine regarding bedtime and sticking to a schedule of going to bed and waking up, there are a few ways of working with your mind that can help.

Writing
Your brain is geared to keep poking at worries like you would a sore tooth. One method of getting it to stop is to write down your concerns and stresses before going to

bed. This is an opportunity to clarify what is bothering you and allows your brain to name it (thus decreasing its power) and to let it go for the night. If you notice the worries intruding when you are trying to sleep, remind yourself that you have it all written down and can now let go and sleep. There is also research showing that writing about stressors helps relieve chronic illness symptoms and pain.

Compassion Practice

Another method of capturing your train of thought in a more helpful way regarding sleep is to use the Loving-Kindness for Others practice in Chapter 3. Focusing your attention on sending compassion to people you care about can automatically calm your brain and relieve your heart.

Relieve Pain

Mind/Body Interventions

Mindfulness and meditation have been mentioned throughout this book. Pain relief is another area where research has shown promising results from meditation practice. While it is difficult to know exactly which aspects of meditation generates reported reductions in pain, some of the psychological effects resulting from the regular practice of meditation are notable in this context.

The increased capacity for emotion regulation resulting from meditation could lessen feelings of chronic pain because it decreases the tendency to become overly focused on painful sensations - often to the exclusion of noticing when you feel pretty good. The nonjudgmental present moment emphasis of meditation can also reduce the tendency to fearfully anticipate future pain , which is called catastrophising.

The Breath Counting meditation in Chapter 5 is a good method for learning how to work with your mind - to pay attention, in the present moment, with a nonjudgmental, inquisitive attitude. With this meditation, when pain is present it can become one aspect of awareness in the midst of a varied field of sensory and cognitive appearances in the mind, thus reducing the way pain dominates your attention.

One participant in my eight week Mindfulness-Based Stress Reduction program reported to the class about her experience regarding pain. She had been taking four to six ibuprofen pills a day for migraine headaches and by the end of the eight weeks, she was not taking any medications. The positive outcomes associated with meditation happen as a result of consistent, regular practice - spending 20 to 30 minutes a day. The point is to become more adept at working with your mind in a new way and to change your relationship with your thoughts, and the positive outcomes are a side effect of that process.

Self-Hypnosis
We all experience pain at some time in our life. It is uncomfortable, and often our psychological fears and the tensing of the muscles around the pain tend to make the discomfort even worse. Self-hypnosis using healing

imagery has been shown to have a positive effect on both the physical signal of pain as well as on our mental reactions.

Hypnosis can be a method to either directly try to reduce the pain through suggestion and imagery or to distract yourself away from noticing the pain. Hypnosis is a method of allowing yourself to relax deeply, which makes your mind more available to suggestions regarding what you would like to have happen. A self-hypnosis script for pain relief follows. You can memorize the gist of the script and guide yourself through envisioning it, or record it for yourself, speaking slowly and allowing many pauses. Alternatively, you could ask someone who has a calming voice to record it for you.

Exercise: Guided Self-Hypnosis for Pain Relief

For the best results, find a quiet place where you will not be disturbed, and sit in a comfortable chair or lie down comfortably and cover yourself, since your body temperature may cool down as you relax. Spend a few moments simply resting and feeling the movements of your breath, and then begin the guided script that follows:

As you rest, imagine yourself standing on a wooded hill, enjoying the forest scents, feeling the pine needle carpet under your feet and the warm light streaming through the treetops. Hear the sounds of birds singing.

Gazing out, you notice a stream at the bottom of the hill. The water sparking in the sunlight draws your attention. As you slowly walk down the hill, you feel yourself getting more and more relaxed with each step, feeling your shoulders and neck muscles softening and releasing as you walk. Each step down the hill brings further comfort and ease.

As you come closer to the stream you notice that the water is very clear, and many healing plants are growing on the sides of the water. There is a mossy section next to the stream where you can comfortably sit. The water looks so appealing that you find yourself reaching out and touching it, noticing it is warm and soothing. Circling your hand gently through the water allows its comforting and healing powers to seep into your hand.

As you continue to soak your hand, the warm comfort begins to extend up your arm and into your shoulders. A soothing feeling moves up into your neck and head, relieving and relaxing all the muscles and nerves as it progresses.

The flow of comfort continues down through your body, easing your breath, and softening your abdomen. Your hips can release any holding, and the soothing comfort can move down each leg. Even your feet let go and relax. Your whole body feels relief and ease. At rest, the flow of comfort goes all through your body. Breathing softly, feel the warm sunlight, the soft air on your face..... (Pause and enjoy this for a few minutes).

As you rest, perhaps you notice a part of your body that may be especially in need of comfort. You can place your hand there, and feel the soothing warmth more directly. Spend as much time as you would like resting and healing......

When you are ready to leave the stream and awaken from this session, do so slowly, gently moving your fingers and toes, opening your eyes and re-orienting yourself to where you are. Remember that you can come back to this healing imagery whenever you wish.

Deep Listening
Another method that I have found helpful for people struggling with pain or chronic conditions is called Deep Listening, and it can help you look more carefully into the psychological components of pain.

The practice of Deep Listening can be helpful for any type of pain. Pain is often a signal or message from the body, and deep listening can help your body communicate with your mind. The following exercise can also be modified to address any chronic illness by focusing on whatever symptoms you experience.

Exercise: Deep Listening

For this exercise, there is no correct answer or specific outcome to be sought. Rather, it is a way of relaxing and allowing images, memories, and thoughts to surface that may usually be out of conscious awareness.

1. Begin by sitting or lying down in a comfortable quiet place where you will not be disturbed. To become more relaxed, practice the square breathing technique introduced in Chapter 1 as follows: Start by noticing your current breathing pattern for a moment. Follow each breath, aware of where it goes and what is moving as you breathe. Then begin counting to four as you breathe in, count to four as you hold your breath, count to four as you release your breath, and then count to four before you breathe in. Keep doing this in an easygoing way until you feel reasonably calm.

2. Now let go of the square breathing technique and bring your attention to a painful place in your body. Without trying to change anything, rest your attention there. Notice what sensations you experience - throbbing, a sharpness, dullness, warmth, coolness... Settle your attention there and really notice what you are experiencing. Are these sensations constant or do they change? Do these sensations stay in one place or do they move? Stay with the sensations for a few moments to see.

3. As you continue to rest your awareness in this place, let your mind drift back, wondering about the first time you experienced these sensations. Do any images, memories or thoughts arise? Just let them be present as you maintain your awareness of your body.

4. As you continue noting the sensations of this place in your body, begin wondering, and perhaps silently even ask your body if it has anything it would like to say to you.

5. Ask your body if there is a way you could help release the pain you have been experiencing.

6. When you have deeply listened as long as you feel it is helpful, thank your body for any guidance you have received and then spend a few minutes simply attending to the sensations of your breath as it moves in and out of your body.

Where pain is concerned, listening to your inner emotional world is important. For example, spine surgeon David Hanscom, MD author of the book *Back in Control: A Spine Surgeon's Road Map Out of Chronic Pain* suggests that there can be a significant psychological component to chronic back pain. Finding new ways to work with anger and anxiety is important, he states, as well as using an integrated approach to build new neural pathways that circumvent the pain. Some of the best tactics noted by Dr. Hanscom include releasing anger and finding forgiveness, and finding a way to play. This, in turn, wakes up the inherent *play pathways* in the brain which can counter the pain pathways. Additionally, a book by Dr. Jeff Brantley entitled *Calming Your Angry Mind: How Mindfulness and Compassion Can Free You From Anger and Bring Peace to Your Life* can be a helpful guide for exploring anger.

Compassion practice is another possibility regarding pain. A group of researchers (Chapin 2014) conducted a pilot study of compassion meditation as an intervention for chronic pain, with positive results. Compassion cultivation has been shown to influence emotional processing and to reduce negativity in the contexts of emotional and physical discomfort, thus suggesting it may be beneficial as a dual treatment for pain and anger. Patients in this study had significantly reduced pain severity and anger and increased pain acceptance at post-treatment compared to treatment baseline. Reviewing the compassion training throughout Chapter 3 can help you with these issues.

Distraction for Pain Relief

You may have observed or read about football players who get injured but keep on playing. This is one of the strongest examples of how distraction can work when pain is present. These players have an overriding interest in what they are doing that allows them to keep going in spite of hurting. If you can find external or internal experiences that are very engaging, it could help you override your own chronic pain in order to do things that you enjoy. Please note I am not recommending harming yourself further when you are experiencing pain, countering your physician's advice, nor ignoring whatever message the pain may be providing.

Here is an example of distraction for pain relief. A young woman had to get a painful spinal injection while in a clinic. The nurse knew she liked horses, and guided her through imagining she was riding in a horse race and had to really focus as she rode the horse over a high jump, just as the spinal procedure was being done. She felt no pain.

What do you find deeply engaging that could help you through either painful procedures or provide a break from chronic pain? It may be an imagined storyline, listening to music, playing an instrument, reading a fascinating tale or talking to a dear friend. It is worth experimenting with new ways to re-engage your mind.

Exercise Motivation
In this chapter we have reviewed ways of caring for your body through nourishing yourself, getting better sleep, and relieving pain. Exercise is also an extremely important factor in caring for your body. Though specific exercise guidance is beyond the scope of this book, I encourage you to find competent people to guide you in whatever exercises are best for you. Look at the American College of Sports Medicine internet reference in the back of this book for more information.

Regarding exercise motivation, however, here are a few points that can boost the likelihood you get to it. One interesting research study reported that people perceived hills to be steeper when they are fatigued relative to when they are well rested (Proffit 1995). Your brain is quite interested in keeping its glucose reserves and seems to deliberately misperceive the difficulty of tasks based on how much glucose is available. Glucose in this case refers to what food turns into for your body to use as energy. Stress depletes energy stores and will contribute to that hill looking higher. When fatigue is diminishing your interest in exercising, choosing and doing one of the stress reduction techniques in this book will help you relieve the fatigue, get a second wind, and feel more capable of keeping those exercise promises you made to yourself.

Another interesting point was made by author Shawn Achor. He calls it the 20 second rule. This "rule" says that if something takes more than 20 seconds to find or prepare for it is less likely that it will get done. In the spirit of this observation he found that going to bed in his exercise clothes made it much more likely he would exercise the next morning upon awakening. Conversely, putting the TV remote in a drawer across the room from the couch will keep your couch potato status to a minimum.

Think through ways you could make it more likely you will keep up your exercise commitments. Keeping exercise clothes and shoes in your car, having a healthy snack available, and getting an exercise buddy who expects you to show up all help to increase the likelihood you will exercise more. Also strategize about ways to enhance the amount of movement you do in an ordinary day. This could be things like walking around your office while on the phone, walking while having meetings, always taking the stairs, and parking farther away from the building.

CHAPTER NINE

REVERSE PLEASURE FATIGUE

Brenda is so very tired of the continual cycle of overeating, dieting, and then starting the whole cycle all over again. Brian finds surfing the internet very stimulating, but in the quiet moments before sleep he feels a vague sense of emptiness and frustration. Charlotte streams a number of television shows and spends many hours sitting in front of the TV, "hooked" on her favorites. Each of these people would tell you that they find their experience of eating, surfing the internet, or watching television as pleasurable. What does that mean?

Pleasure

A psychologist might describe pleasure as a positive feedback mechanism, motivating you to recreate in the future the situation which you have just found pleasurable. This sounds innocent enough - you experience something you like and are very interested in recreating it again - but there is a catch. This brain paradigm was established when we lived in a long ago world where pleasures were somewhat rare and fleeting, not our current situation where a vast array of pleasures are at our beck and call 24 hours a day. Think about the convenience stores, grocery stores, bars, shopping malls, movie theaters, television shows, movies on demand, and on and on.

Our brains have not been able to keep up with the incredible increase in access to pleasure that we have in modern society. As was mentioned in the Care for Your Body chapter, refined sugar is not something that occurs in nature, so the human brain developed to respond strongly on the rare occasions when an intense sweetness, such as honey, was available. The internal commentary is something like "this is great, more would be even better," and there doesn't seem to be a turn off switch. So even though sugar is available to us everywhere we turn, our brains continue to treat it as a rare and highly desirable substance - and Brenda keeps going through cycles of overeating and then intense calorie restriction.

If food is not what lights up your pleasure centers, then perhaps it is entertainment, shopping, alcohol, drugs, or gambling, all of which are also easily available to us. Most of us have access to constant entertainment on television, or are hooked on the excitement of hearing the "ping" of a new message on the computer. Regarding computer use, Gary Small in Scientific American Mind (2008), named this thriving on perpetual connectivity "techno-brain burnout," because over time the results are impaired cognition, depression, and the actual re-shaping of our brain structure. People who compulsively use the internet are reporting withdrawal symptoms of anger, depression, and irritability when the internet is inaccessible - just like addicts report when separated from their substance of choice. This is the situation Brian finds himself in, but he doesn't know what to do about it.

Years of working with people in my psychotherapy practice and in the workshops I teach has led me to apply the umbrella term pleasure fatigue for this pervasive syndrome. Pleasure fatigue is when pleasure itself, because of overuse, has a diminished capacity to perform in the same physiological and or psychological way it once did, resulting in a yearning for and an increased effort to gain the previous levels of pleasant experience. Pleasure fatigue is showing up in a wide range of domains. As mentioned earlier, one of the most obvious is the area of food consumption. Food manufacturers know that our pleasure centers can not only be engaged, but actually hooked by well-researched combinations of sugar, fat and salt. Then, the ordinary pleasure derived from the sweetness of non-processed foods such as fruit, can no longer compete.

It is not that pleasures are bad, it is that you get trapped in a mind state of thinking of the next pleasure before you have even finished the current one. I distinctly remember biting into a particularly appealing macaroon, all soft and chewy, and before even finishing the first bite I was looking around to see if there were any more. This strong sense of being compelled to experience more and more pleasure keeps the mind stirred up, and keeps your psyche consumed with constant wanting. You then miss opportunities to experience your innate capability to have a mental state that is clear, open and calm - which is the ultimate pleasure. The following exercise is one way of examining pleasure.

Exercise: Free Reign

For this next exercise to be most effective, it is important to *do the first part before reading the directions for the second part.*

Part I: Sit in a quiet place with a pen and 2 pieces of paper. For several minutes, on the first piece of paper, write down whatever comes to mind that you desire. Write "I want:" and then go for it, listing whatever arises. There are no restrictions regarding cost, no reality check. Use both sides of the paper if you need to.

When you are finished, put down the pen and read over your list. Then close your eyes, and tune in to your body. How does it feel? How is your state of mind - stirred up, calm, anxious, excited? How do you feel about having this particular list of wants?

Part II: Sit in a quiet place with a pen and the second piece of paper. Spend a moment just focusing on your breath, allowing it to help you feel at ease. Then bring your awareness into your chest, your "heart center."

Relax your body and breathe into this area for a moment. Feeling your heart center, again write *from my heart I want*, and make a list of whatever comes to mind. When you are finished, tune in to your body and your state of mind. Then compare the two lists.

For many people there is a marked difference between the two lists. When we focus only from the chin up, we may be like greedy children, wanting everything in sight. However, when we tune into our heart, our more deeply held values, we can remember to focus on what is really important to us.

The ancient philosopher Epicurus stated that the definition of pleasure was *to be free from turmoil in the soul.* Look closely at the ways you seek pleasure - are they false refuges or do they bring peace to your mind and true satisfaction to your life? The choice is yours.

Psychological Prosperity
Most of us feel that monetary wealth would bring happiness, and it does most likely increase our standard of living and make life easier. However we often overlook *psychological prosperity*, which can also result in feelings of wellbeing. In the research of Ed Diener (2010), psychological prosperity was described as including such things as learning, autonomy, using one's skills, respect, and the ability to count on others in an emergency. Examine your life and appreciate or seek these opportunities to feel psychological prosperity. Con-

templating the psychological prosperity exercise that
follows will help you.

Exercise: Psychological Prosperity

Examine your life in light of the concept of psychological
prosperity. It can help you appreciate what you already
have or provide guidance for a happier, more fulfilled
future.

1. What are the opportunities in your life for continued
learning in areas that interest you?

- at home

- at work

- at school or in continuing education

- in the local community in venues such as art centers,
museums, senior groups, meet ups...

2. Are there new and interesting ways you could use the skills you already have?

- at work

- at home

- in the community or neighborhood

- in groups such as the chamber of commerce, art centers, volunteer groups, and clubs

3. Contemplate respect. Are your interactions with others, behaviors, and lifestyle choices worthy of respect? Do you feel good about the way others view you?

4. Make a list of the ways you can count on others to help you when needed.

- relatives

- co-workers

- friends

- neighbors

- local organizations

5. Ponder the following questions regarding psychological prosperity:

- Do you need to appreciate and reinforce existing relationships?

- Do you need to cultivate new connections?

- Are you someone others can rely on in times of need?

Recognizing opportunities to realize psychological prosperity will not happen all at once. This can be a lifelong interest for continuing growth.

Happiness
Another way of sorting out the effects of pleasure in our life is to distinguish the types of happiness we seek. We could distinguish two basic forms of well-being: a "hedonic" form, which are positive emotions from self-gratifying experiences, and a deeper "eudaimonic" form that results from striving toward meaning and a noble purpose beyond simple self-gratification. The word

eudaimonic is originally from a Greek system of ethics which notes that good actions will produce happiness. Interestingly, the word roots are "eu" meaning well, and "daimonic" meaning guardian spirit.

Researcher Barbara Fredrickson (2013) looked at genetic responses to these two forms of happiness. In this research there is preliminary evidence that eudaimonic well-being (looking toward meaning and a higher purpose) predicted a more favorable pattern of gene expression than did hedonic well-being. The results indicate that striving toward higher goals could stimulate a greater health producing genetic transcription regarding inflammation than happiness derived from self-gratification. In other words, how you choose to seek happiness has an effect on your genetic makeup. Those pleasures connected with deeper meaning are more likely to enhance your health.

If you are someone who is experiencing pleasure fatigue, feeling hooked, dependent, and driven to do the same thing over and over again, not only to feel some level of pleasure, but to avoid the slump or depression that results from not carrying out the same activities, there is a possibility for change.

There are ways to re-set your pleasure gauge, whereby you can feel more in control of your mind and body, and once again enjoy the ordinary pleasures life offers. A study combining results from 51 randomized controlled interventions found that people prompted to engage in positive intentional activities, such as thinking gratefully, optimistically, or mindfully, became significantly happier (Sin and Lyubomirsky 2009). The exercise that follows can help you intentionally improve your well-being. It is important for you to choose what you would enjoy doing, as taking these on as a duty or out of obligation will not help.

Exercise: Apply Pleasure Fatigue Antidotes

- Recognize that human desires are endless, and chasing after them is like drinking salt water - the more you drink the thirstier you become.

- Contemplate what is worth seeking. Can you devote more time to fulfilling what is most important to you?

- Experiment with your own brain's pleasure responses. Studies show that the same pleasure centers that are stimulated by vices are also awakened by virtues such as meditation, voluntary exercise, and prayer.

- Acts of kindness and giving to charity also tend to bring about a pleasure response.

- Note time for positive activities on your daily schedule in the same way you would schedule events and responsibilities.

- Purposely attend to something you love - a person, sports activity, your garden, or a pet.

- Awaken your senses and take mental note when in the presence of ordinary sights, sounds, smells and tastes you enjoy.

- Spend a few minutes each day in "Aimless Wandering." Drop any agenda and relax by strolling in the beauty of nature.

- When positive experiences occur, spend at least 10 seconds appreciating them, which alerts the brain to enjoy and to remember what is happening.

- Keep a log or diary of pleasant experiences, which not only helps you appreciate them, but also can provide further pleasure when you later re-read what you noted.

- Write letters expressing gratitude.

Exercise: Abundance Breathing

This is an easy exercise that can be done any time in order to experience a more relaxed state of mind. Begin by focusing on your breath for a moment. Then as you continue, contemplate the notion that the air you breathe, the most fundamental support of your life, is freely available. It is there in whatever quantity you need, whenever you want it. Feel how miraculous that is, and spend a few moments experiencing your breath with gratitude and appreciation.

Exercise: Pleasure Noting

Keep a pen and a sheet of paper or a small notebook with you for one week. Every time something pleasant occurs - no matter how small - write it down. Review your list at the end of each day. What is the balance between the ordinary pleasures that are part of life, and the ones you seek that are perhaps not so healthy? It is helpful to consciously take note of all the usually overlooked opportunities to feel good in a healthy way that happen every day.

Exercise: Self Inquiry

Spend some time contemplating and writing down answers to the following questions:

- If I had to describe my life in 3 sentences what would they be?

- What activities lift my spirit?

- If I had a week of no work and no electronics (TV, phone, computer, etc.) what would I do with my time?

- What are my three most important values? Values can be in areas such as family, community, environment, self, and work. Some specific examples of values include responsibility, service, honesty, collaboration, stewardship, independence, integrity, enjoyment, security, learning, accomplishment, loyalty, compassion, generosity, dependability, and wisdom.

- Am I living according to my most important values?

- What does contentment mean to me?

- Create a mission statement regarding your life.

It is easy in our materialistic culture to get swept up in a sea of possessions and become swayed away from our basic values. Doing a values re-assessment now and again can provide the ground for a more sane and happy life.

CHAPTER TEN

BUILD YOUR RESOURCES

Self Esteem

I work with many people who have low self esteem. They have a long list of reasons why they are just not good enough. Not feeling good about yourself has consequences. You may think you are not worthy of respect, making it easier for others to take advantage of you. For example, do you find yourself frequently saying yes to requests when you really want to say no (and thereby not having time to do what is important for yourself)? If you are very self critical, it may lead to you avoiding taking social risks and unnecessarily restricting your life, which can contribute to unhappiness.

Exercise: Build Self-Esteem

One way of building self esteem is to deliberately recognize all the best qualities of yourself that often go overlooked.   In each of the following categories write down ways you contribute or can feel good about these areas of your life.   For example, at home perhaps you keep a nice yard, or help your children with their homework, make the lunches, or keep the family budget. Maybe you volunteer in the community or are a contributing member of your church or spiritual group. Don't be shy about recognizing the many ways you create enjoyment, take care of basic needs, or make the world a better place.

• Friendships:

• Work:

• Creativity:

• Self-care:

• Community:

- Spiritual life:

- Family:

- Volunteer:

- Hobbies/talents:

We often overlook everyday ways we make life interesting, more meaningful, or even possible for others, or ways we take care of our own health and wellbeing that are important. Take note and give yourself a pat on the back.

Foundational Relationships
Foundational relationships in this context means the people in your life that you rely on. These could be family, friends, or co-workers. Do you actively cultivate these relationships, or do you take them for granted? Keeping good foundational relationships is very

important to your own wellbeing. It does not necessarily require a big time commitment, but it does require regular attention.

A few simple ways of keeping up your foundational relationships are as follows:

- Put important dates on your calendar, such as birthdays and anniversaries of friends and relatives, and honor these days in some way.

- Use Skype to keep up with family and friends who live at a distance.

- Send a small gift out of the blue occasionally to people who are important to you.

- Thank people who do things for you day to day that you may usually overlook.

- If you are in a marriage or partnership, spend at least a half an hour a day doing something that will please that other person - even if it is just picking up the dry cleaning, or taking a walk with them.

- Apologize for hurting others.

Perspective

I once asked a friend the following question: *If you could do whatever you wanted, without restrictions such as cost, or family obligations, work or time restraints, what would you do?* Take a moment to contemplate this question for yourself.

My friend answered that she would like to paint by the seashore. By doing this exercise, she recognized that what she most wanted to do was actually accessible for her, at least for a week, and she did it. We often feel so hemmed in by our life that we forget that we can still not only dream, but also realize our dream in some measure. Recognizing this can lift your spirit and provide something very positive for moving forward.

Renewal

Every so often it is worth spending time reviewing your life and renewing your commitment to your own wellbeing. This could be done at the new year or perhaps on your birthday. One form this could take is as follows:

1. Reflect on your actions through the previous year. Have there been times when you acted in a harmful way to yourself or to others? Admitting your mistakes with a sense of regret (rather than guilt) is very relieving. Regret reflects an acceptance of the fact that human beings make mistakes, whereas guilt tends to feel more like a sense of personal inadequacy.

2. Reflect on how you might act differently in the future. Bring in what you have learned about Conscious Benevolence. Can you apply self-kindness and a forgiving heart?

3. Write down the positive qualities you would like to embody going forward. Contemplate how you will integrate these qualities into your daily life.

This renewal process can be done for yourself, or can be done in a group or with your family. If this feels valuable, you could also make it a daily practice before going to bed.

A Final Note
I am hoping that through reading this book you have gotten new insights into how to take care of yourself in unique and powerful ways. You might consider making copies of some of the exercises that you would like to repeat and keeping them in an easily accessible place. Practices such as meditation and loving-kindness can lead you on a very positive lifelong journey into the depths of your own consciousness as well as into new ways of relating to others and to the world. I hope you will find ways of integrating the practices that "speak" to you into your everyday life.

May you be well, peaceful, and at ease.

RESOURCES

BOOKS

Benson H. and Proctor W. 2010. *Relaxation Revolution: enhancing your personal health through the science and genetics of mind body healing.* Scribner, NY.

Brantley, J. 2014. *Calming Your Angry Mind: how mindfulness and compassion can free you from anger and bring peace to your life.* New Harbinger, Oakland, CA.

Hanscom, D. 2012. *Back in Control: a spine surgeon's roadmap out of chronic pain.* Vertus Press, Seattle.

Khalsa, S. 2000. *Breathwalk: breathing your way to a revitalized body, mind and spirit.* Random House, NY.

Loring, S. 2010. *Eating with Fierce Kindness: a mindful and compassionate guide to losing weight.* New Harbinger, Oakland, CA.

Neff, K. 2011. *Self-Compassion: the proven power of being kind to yourself.* HarperCollins, NY.

Wansink, B. 2006. *Mindless Eating: why we eat more than we think.* Bantam Dell, NY.

INTERNET EDUCATION

growwellnc.com. Behavior changes for healthier living.
www.acsm.org/access-public-information. The American
College of Sports Medicine website.

RESEARCH REFERENCES

Bob, P. et al. 2013. Conscious attention, meditation, and
bilateral information transfer. *Clinical EEG and
Neuroscience* Vol. 44(1), 39-43.

Breines J. et al. 2014. Self-compassion as a predictor of
interleukin-6 response to acute psychosocial stress.
Brain, Behavior, and Immunity, Vol. 37, 109–114.

Cahill, L. et al. 2013. Skipping breakfast or eating late at
night increases risk of coronary heart disease.
Circulation 128(4) 337-43.

Carson, JW. et al. 2010. A pilot randomized controlled
trial of the Yoga of Awareness program in the
management of fibromyalgia. *Pain*, Vol. 151(2). 530-539.

Chapin, H. et al. 2014. Pilot study of a compassion
meditation intervention in chronic pain.   *Journal of
Compassionate Health Care*, 1(4).

Colantuoni, C. et al. 2002. Evidence that intermittent, excessive sugar intake causes endogenous opioid dependence. *Obesity Research*, Vol. 10 (6), 478-488.

Crum, A. and Langer, E. 2007. Mind set matters: exercise and the placebo effect. *Psychological Science,* Vol. 18 (2), 165-171.

Diener, E. et al. 2010. Wealth and happiness across the world: material prosperity predicts life evaluation whereas psychosocial prosperity predicts positive feeling. *Journal of Personality and Social Psychology*, Vol. 99(1) 52-61.

Fredrickson, B. et al. 2008. Open hearts build lives: positive emotions, induced through loving-kindness meditation, build consequential personal resources. *Journal of Personality and Social Psychology.* 95: 1045-62.

Fredrickson, B. 2013. Functional genomic perspective on human well-being. *Crossmark,* Vol. 110(33),13684-13689.

Froeliger, B. Garland, E. and McClernon, J. 2012. Yoga meditation practitioners exhibit greater grey matter volume and fewer reported cognitive failures: results of a preliminary voxel-based morphometric analysis. *Evidence-Based Complementary and Alternative Medicine.*

Goleman, D. 2003. The lama in the lab. *Shambhala Sun.*

Hoge, E. et al. 2013. Loving-Kindness Meditation practice associated with longer telomeres in women. *Brain, Behavior, and Immunity*, Vol. 32 , 159-163.

Holman, et al. 2013. Media's role in broadcasting acute stress following the Boston Marathon bombings. *CrossMark,* vol. 3(1), E.A. 93-98.

Jalal, D. et al. 2010. Increased fructose associates with elevated blood pressure. *Journal of the American Society of Nephrology.* Vol. 21(9).

Kaptchuk, TJ. et al. 2010. Placebos without deception: a randomized controlled trial in irritable bowel syndrome *PLoS one.*

Kaptchuk, TJ. et al. 2008. Components of placebo effect: randomized controlled trial in patients with irritable bowel syndrome. *BMJ.*

Larsson, S. et al. 2006. Consumption of sugar and sugar-sweetened foods and the risk of pancreatic cancer in a prospective study. *The American Journall of Clinical Nutrition*, vol. 84 (5).

Lenoir, M. et al. 2007. Intense sweetness surpasses cocaine reward. *PloS one.*

Levinson, DB. et al. 2014. A mind you can count on: validating breath counting as a behavioral measure of mindfulness, *Frontiers in Psychology* 5: 1202.

McCubbin, T. et al. 2014. Mindfulness-based stress reduction in an integrated care delivery system : one-year impacts on patient-centered outcomes and health care utilization. *The Permanente Journal* Vol. 18(4).

Neff, K. and R. Vonk. 2008. Self-compassion versus global self-esteem: Two different ways of relating to oneself. *Journal of Personality.* 77: 23-60.

O'Connor, DB. et al. 2008. Effects of daily hassles and eating style on eating behavior. *Health Psychology,* Vol. 27.

Proffitt DR. 1995. Perceiving geographical slant. *Psychonomic Bulletin & Review.* 2(4):409–428.

Sin N. L. and S. Lyubomirsky. 2009. Enhancing well-being and alleviating depressive symptoms with positive psychology interventions: A practice friendly meta-analysis. *Journal of Clinical Psychology.* 65, 467–487.

Small, G. 2008. Your iBrain: how technology changes the way we think. *Scientific American Mind.* Oct/Nov.

Trakhtenberg, EC. 2008. The effects of guided imagery on the immune system: a critical review. *International Journal of Neuroscience,* Vol. 118(6).

ABOUT THE AUTHOR

Sasha Loring, M.Ed, LCSW is an experienced psychotherapist, stress management consultant, and mindfulness teacher. She has provided consultations at Duke Integrative Medicine, Duke Executive Health Clinic, Duke Diet and Fitness Center and in a private psychotherapy practice. She has taught courses at a range of venues including Glaxo Pharmaceutical, Omega Institute, University of North Carolina Integrative Medicine, Duke Medical Center, Sivananda Yoga Retreat Center, and meditation centers around the country. She teaches the Mindfulness-Based Stress Reduction Program and Mindful Eating workshops. She has been featured on the radio and in the Wall Street Journal, eMindful website, and on BBC Television.

More information can be found at www.sashaloring.com

NOTES

RELIEF

Made in the USA
Middletown, DE
31 March 2015